HE PETERS BLACK AND BLUE GUIDE TO CURRENT LITERARY JOURNALS

With drawings
by
MEREDITH PETERS

Cherry Valley Editions
1983

Drawings throughout by Meredith Peters

Copyright c 1983 Robert Peters

Copyright c 1983 Meredith Peters

First edition.

ACKNOWLEDGEMENTS

The following pieces appeared in a raccoon monograph: Antaeus, APR, Chelsea, Field, Iowa Review, and Southern Review.

The New Yorker appeared in Boxcar; Pushcart Poetry in Contact II.

Library of Congress Cataloging in Publication Data

Peters, Robert, 1924-
    The Peters black and blue guide to current literary
        journals.

    Includes index.
    1. American poetry--Periodicals--History.
2. American periodicals--History. 3. American poetry
20th century--History and criticism. I. Title.
PS580.P47 1983   811'.008   83-1993
ISBN 0-916156-66-4

Cherry Valley Editions
are distributed by:

Writers & Books
892 S. Clinton Ave.
Rochester, N.Y. 14620

JOURNALS EXAMINED

"the reverent reader may
haply find himself on the high
road to distraction, the
irreverent will too probably
find himself on the verge of
laughter."

    --A.C. Swinburne, "Wordsworth & Byron" 1884

BLESSINGS OBLIQUE AND DIRECT

"That day there were too many words."--<u>Alison</u> <u>Turner</u>,
    HUDSON REVIEW

"What blazes the trail is not necessarily pretty."--<u>Mary</u>
    <u>Oliver</u>, GEORGIA REVIEW.

"The stones are gray / and so are they."--<u>Robert</u>
    <u>Francis</u>, FIELD.

"I work a slick witchcraft that joins to beauty."--
    Frederick<u>Morgan</u>, HUDSON REVIEW.

"The heavy burden of the tune...hums us to the grave."--
    <u>John</u> <u>Hollander</u>, ANTAEUS.

"I like the way a redneck dances."--<u>Mary</u> <u>Ann</u> <u>McFadden</u>,
    KAYAK.

"Nobody would call it poetry."--<u>Stephen</u> <u>Berg</u>, PUSHCART.

"I feel a measure of guilt."--<u>Thomas</u> <u>Swiss</u>, IOWA REVIEW.

INTRODUCTION

The risks I take in compiling this Guide are considerable. Not only do I risk offending two score or more editors of some of our most enduring magazines; my criticisms may also sit badly with poets. A wiser critic would, perhaps, be more circumspect. But to throw bouquets at these journals would be mere sycophancy. I realize that it is always easy to fuss and blow whistles; to chop down an oak is much easier than to plant a new one.

My design has been to open with observations on a particular journal, and then scrutinize the poets showcased. In the interests of space, I exclude fiction, essays, and most of the reviews. This has been a difficult decision, for, God knows, a similar assessment of the prose, particularly of the fiction, is needed. I do scan reviews towards determining the degree to which these magazines are creatures of trade and university presses. Alas, if you publish with alternative presses, your chances of being reviewed are almost nil. The large presses are the ones that buy the ad space. THE AMERICAN BOOK REVIEW is the only widely distributed journal in the country representing small presses with some regularity and gusto. And THE SMALL PRESS REVIEW, while devoted to the interests of alternative publishers, devotes too little space to reviews.

For the most part, I have scrutinized only one issue (the most recent I could find) of each journal. My principle is that you can tell the breed of the hen by examining a few feathers, either off or on the bird. I had first intended to parallel the famous Michelin Travel Guides, awarding crossed pens (instead of knives and forks or miniscule hotels) for achievement, or lack thereof. The Michelin Company, alas, refused to grant permission for me to use their logo, deciding, I assume that to risk offending a single potential purchaser of their tires is bad business. May their M. Pneu lie down on a bed of nails! Meredith Peters, whose graphics are well-known in the alternative press world, has supplied the drawings scattered throughout the book.

If I can manage to alert a few readers to what is really going on in the world of the Established Literary Magazine, I shall be satisfied. Perhaps I may even inspire an editor or two to be more cautious about the work he or she accepts. Some readers may cancel their subscriptions. Teachers may stop using the periodicals in their classes. A handful of writers may desist from concocting the pablum most of these editors appear to favor. Perhaps yearly Guides will appear, revisiting these journals and adding new ones. As M. Michelin Pneu says: "<u>Vos avis et suggestions</u> seront <u>les</u> bienvenus <u>pour</u> <u>compléter</u> <u>nos</u> <u>informations</u> <u>et</u> <u>rectifier,</u> <u>s'il</u> <u>y</u> <u>a</u> <u>lieu,</u> <u>nos</u> <u>judgements.</u>"

   I seek poems that excite with zest, passion, and originality. I don't care how old, or how new, the forms. I admire pieces as old-fashioned as Brooks Haxton's mock-epic "Breakfast Ex Animo," from POETRY, or David Ray's dramatic monologue, "Richard St. George, Esquire, Orders His Portrait from Henry Fuseli, 1791," from THE GEORGIA REVIEW. And I like the fresh work of younger, randy poets (viz., those appearing in LITTLE CAESAR and THE WORMWOOD REVIEW). I protest Academic Sleaze in any of its numerous guises. Moss grows on one side of a tree; sleaze covers its host completely. I also dislike Momentosity, when an uninspired poet, often famous, is pompous, conceptual, and abstract. A related malady arises from the use of frayed, bilious, exhausted imitations of Shakespeare. And there are other features greatly suspect: insipid line-breaks to decoy readers from an insipid content; the endless fascination with the trivial--an obsession with belly-button fuzz. Then there is the "Thoreau Poem," related to the "Robert Frost" poem, which evokes little spiritual moments vapidly assembled, along with the mushrooms, chigger bites, and skunk urine. I hope to encourage better writing, whether it be anachronistic or experimental.

   I wish to report, finally, that I keep a stack of recapped Michelins inside my front door, and own a M. Pneu costume. So, potentially disgruntled poet or editor, be warned, if you should appear wishing for fisticuffs!

ABRAXAS

Nos. 25/26(1982). Editors: Ingrid Swanberg, Warren Woessner. 2518 Gregory St., Madison, WI 53711. 4 issues for $8.

There's a lot of poetry here--140 pages worth, including a feature on 58 Wisconsin poets. 104 poets in all. Some of these writers are good. In general, the editors like experiential poems tinged with funk, à la Bukowski, Locklin, D. R. Wagner, and Hugh Fox.

Douglas Blazek opens with a sinister little Surrealist poem about men in "a subliminal room" committing mayhem on a severed head. The poor thing has its eyes gouged out with a potato peeler, its nose shattered with a hammer, and a mop handle shoved through both ears. The head resurrects. T. L. Kryss displays a rat who visits his family on Christmas Eve, bearing gifts of stunned creatures fetched from city sewers. A set of unicorns visit a wooden Christ and lick its feet. D. R. Wagner writes an expansive love poem with a grisly touch--"The Body of Dream in Autopsy." The Surrealism seems casual and frayed. Here's a Kleenex Poem, a throwaway piece, by William Cochran, meant for one reading: "DOING CHORES"

> You get this mess cleaned up right now
> screamed mother what are you pigs?
>
> Yes mother yes we squealed.

Editor Warren Woessner observes wild-life in transit: Kids, on Halloween, contribute joint-smells to fall-woodsmoke. Mourning doves leave their cedar tree roosts. A hawk diving for a dove stuns itself on the ground:

> Solid thud, hawk
> diving after a dove, stunned
> spreadeagled on the ground--
> cat food, surely as the dove was yours.
> It was my glass
> you took for sky,
> so I kicked cat back got gloves
> and set you on the toolshed roof.
> One flap later you were gone.
> No thanks but mine, I guess
> that I could touch you,
> look you in the eye,

12

and someday, beauty,
see you kill again.

Joe Bruchac writes sentimentally about Vietnam's
adolescent boy-soldiers, providing a pastiche of Indian
lads (Lakotas or Iroquois), the Cambodians and
Vietnamese, and ancient Khmer lancers. This oleo
doesn't spread well. There are six vintage Bukowski
poems, with drawing. Here's "one for the dark":

I slept through the sixties
I slept through the seventies

I'm sleeping now

don't wake me up

the light hurts my eyes
the faces hurt my eyes

sleep beats anything
showing

don't wake me up.

Gerald Locklin loads in some Locklinean wisdom: "she
learned a lot in the school / of hard knocks. . .it's an
/ entirely male faculty." Vitality via David Maurice,
cartoon and poem. Hugh Fox uses jazz rhythms to evoke a
father leaning over sick child:

Kit-Kat
little ragged rat
belly-sleep sprawled 3 AM small
in the middle of his immense
crib,
"Are you Daddy's
big boy....are you going
to grow up to be
a big guy....?"
the nightclubish-subdued red
and cream nightlights
fanwhirr
the bubbling of the
humidifier

Heavy-Metal Symbolism from Richard Kostelanetz' white
page with gold, silver, bronze, and lead. You go around
his piece, as you might traverse the lid of a shoebox.
Will Inman rifts poems with undercurrents of rage,
violence, sex, and sentimentality: "i am hammering
turquoise / into the sockets of my hate," Inman's irate
speaker declares to Estaban (a lover?) who seems to have
gone back to his wife. Less of a screaming piece is

"Territories and Realms," which reviews the faded topic of women seeking to become warriors. Feeling and brains appear in Duane Locke's poem about Apuleius' frescoes. John Yamrus contributes a trite love poem--he kisses his lady's mouth and feels "the tender little paradise" of her leg on his. Roger Pfingston writes unpretentiously about a sing-along with a cricket.

The Wisconsin poems are recommended. As one might expect, rural landscapes dominate. All poets eschew bravura writing, and there are no well-wrought poems (imitations of past forms). The language is direct, simple, and denotative. John Cort's romp with tripled (but uncompleted) parentheses is a contrast with most of the other work here:

```
(the Indo-Gangetic Plain
(was once a forest
    ((the Indus Valley civilization
    ((deforested itself
    ((the rivers moved
    ((dried up
    ((the abandoned cities
    ((died...
```

If you remember ABRAXAS as one of the more iconoclastic magazines of the sixties, you will feel comfortable that many of those talents, now quickly aging (Bukowski, Locklin, Blazek, Lifshin, etc.), are still writing much as they were then. A déja vu! Where are the young outrageous writers these days?

THE AMERICAN POETRY REVIEW

Vol.11:1(Jan. 1982). Editors: Stephen Berg, Arthur Vogelsang, et al. 1616 Walnut St., Room 405, Philadelphia, PA 19103. $7.50 per year.

A fellow-poet who would probably be pleased to be named, once characterized THE AMERICAN POETRY REVIEW as being as "persistent as THE WATCHTOWER." I love that. While hucksters don't stand on street corners or at shopping malls with copies of APR, the tabloid seems ubiquitous. Even a disaffected former subscriber who asked for a refund on the remainder of his subscription monies (he was informed that no refunds are made), choosing to live out his days without ever again seeing

APR, finds that it keeps turning up. It stares out from
friends' coffee tables. Sample copies appear at the
University where he teaches. Anxious MFA poets, with
inky hands, display the latest glamorous hype-photo for
some poet they know featured on the cover of APR. Well,
what do we get from the tabloid? I shall scrutinize
this recent issue, one that turned up the other day in
my campus mail.

Two long poems by Laurence Lieberman lead off.
Both manifest energy and some good and some awful
writing. A Japanese tilemaker caps his thirty years of
crafting with a temple built on a steep bluff. He's the
"impresario of the hill, / the happy tile-Czar" who
directs a protégé's movements on the heights. So far so
good. What hurts is the sudden irruption of clichés:
"he breaks new ground...he takes risks...his eyes glow."
Lieberman's problem, I think, is that he can't make up
his mind whether to be the tilemaker or the observer.
Alas, he keeps intruding with less than inspired
observations: "Ah, slowly he creeps into his roof- /
walker's second skin of an artist!" The old man has a
"keen tilist eye." His disciple "may carry / into the
future" this man's Cézanne-skill. (It helps, so
Lieberman fancies, that the old man spent years in
France, as a youth, and discovered Cézanne, who became
"his patron saint."). And Lieberman's clumsy forcing of
the art-notions doesn't help, viz.: "Now he infuses into
body language of his delivery hand-wafts / of dance
choreographer, / lilted gestures of band conductor on
his podium, or opera / scenarist molding stage sets /
(he has studied their styles in theatre rehearsals)...."
This is cluttered. It's as if Lieberman has pocketed the
old man's jockstrap with heavy stones, impeding thereby
his attack on "his canvas / the many-layered sweep of
hillslopes."

Lieberman's second poem, "Eros at the World Kite
Pageant," I am happy to note, has fewer clichés; the
event is more leanly handled--the style is less self-
conscious, and there's verve: "outright / sodomy"
transpires in the air.

The ever-burgeoning Rilke industry is served by
eight poems stodgily translated by Stephen Mitchell.
Rilke should look down from heaven and, after a certain
number, say 52, of his orts have been skewered in a
single year, should shout "Halt!" and jab out the eyes
of the translator busy on the 53rd poem. I urge him to
jab out the eyes with rose thorns. After all,
translating dead poets is a form of necrophilia.

Joan Murray, nicely photographed against slender
tree-trunks, spins those first-person riffs so admired

by the editors of APR. She's predictable--a cicada "cuts
the elm like a chain saw." Katydids argue "the same
position summer after summer." Murray interlards her
dulling first-person takes with momentous-sounding,
fancy writing. When she sees a neighbor kid pin a
wriggling horseshoe crab to his shed, she observes that
it is not for her "to think / of prying the nailed
carapace / from the weathered planks." She'll let it
hang there "like any god."

Despite brownie points earned at the KENYON, NEW
ENGLAND, and VIRGINIA QUARTERLY REVIEWS, Carol Frost,
although trivial, is sophisticated. Should she fetch
brown eggs from her henyard to her kitchen? Robert
Louthan, complete with macho pool-table photo, caroms
his poems with a certain panache and veils his personal
obsessions behind other voices: a ventriloquist's dummy;
a husband waiting to break out of his coffin to bug his
wife once more; and a "testimonial" to a lost soul who
attends too many poetry readings. Harold Levy,
recipient of a 1980 CAPS Fellowship, writes easy poems
tacked down with the sort of allusions that go over big
in workshops--to the painter Masaccio, to Spanish poets,
to New Orleans jazz.

More translations follow, of Gunter Grass and
Elizabeth Borchers. Finally, we reach the back page,
and a poem, "Fairyland," by Robert Pinsky. Seen in a
white, open-throated shirt, hand in pocket, loins tipped
slightly forward, Pinsky is smiling and casual. His
poem, though, lacks his charm. There's too much "fur
and absurd finery" in "Fairyland." A tired ear settles
for facile sounds: "our most ancient decayed hope / Is a
gross infantile greed." More stones weight Apollo's
celestial jockstrap. The fairy of poetry didn't stroke
Pinsky quite enough with his/her magical wand. One
hopes for much more.

One thing that jolts me about APR, something I
hadn't really observed before, is how much it appears
the creature of large trade and university presses. Here
are the trade publishers featured in this issue:
Pinsky's publisher is Princeton; translator Steven
Polgar belongs to Harper & Row: James Wright was at home
at Random House, as is Stephen Mitchell (and at Penquin,
Grove, and Doubleday); Lieberman is published by
Macmillan. Murray and Frost appear in staid,
establishment poetry journals. Louthan alone is
published by a small press, Alice James. He is the best
poet in the issue.

If one examines the books reviewed, the same
pattern emerges. The ubiquitous Dave Smith, whose
recent University of Illinois book is reviewed here by

Stephen Yensur, writes a portmanteau piece on 15 poetry books. 14 of these are published by trade or university presses (5 come from Princeton). Sandra McPherson examines Ted Hughes' MOORTOWN, courtesy of Harper & Row. Readers may care to examine the ads. Suffice it to say, if you hope to appear in APR, credentials will help, preferably ones with conservative literary magazines, or with trade and university presses. So, is APR our poetry WATCHTOWER, meant for those really needing salvation? I fear not! Perhaps Berg and Vogelsang should set out soon on a journey to Emmaeus. Something might then just change...for the better. But don't be too hopeful.

ANTAEUS

No. 44 (Winter 1982). Editor: Daniel Halpern. Ecco Press, 18 West 30th St., New York, NY 10001. $14 Annual Subscription.

I face ANTAEUS apprehensively, expecting to find therein more of the dullness characterizing other Ecco efforts--the National Poetry Series and the publications of the Ecco Press itself. No literary magazine in America has so many bases covered--European poetry, English poetry, American poetry, living poets, old poets, young poets, interviews, documents left behind by dead poets. The grandeur is intimidating, as was the Libyan giant, Antaeus, a bully who passed through the countryside looking for fights. As long as he kept touching Mother Earth, he remained invincible. That Arnold Schwarzenegger of his age, Hercules, found out the bully's secret, held him above the Earth and crushed him.

H.D, the current darling of mags with a necrophiliac bent, treats us to laminated myths of sex and life, executed with her usual mix of tedium and energy. This set of pieces ("Sigil VIII-XIX") is fragmentary, in the way that classical statues are. How appropriate! All through, these fragments are despoiled (deflowered) by inept generalizations--God, the future, the past, cycles of history.... All the while, H. D. aches quite simply to bury her face in her lover's pussy. H.D. is seldom entirely up-front though, and hides her eroticism behind Greeky touches, Delphi-isms. (This is what poets had to do in her day, so I must not be too severe). H.D. was ice, the lover was fire. She fantasizes the pair soaring above the Symplegedes, "wing-tip to purple wing," creating "new" skies and

earth. Finally, she wants her "wild heart" beaten to
death. What she proffers is imitative <u>Francis Thompson</u>,
tinged with lesbian eroticism. Her <u>Bitch of Heaven</u>
pursueth H.D. through labyrinthine days and ways,
evoking some sound, some fury.

<u>William</u> <u>Stafford</u> is good in "For A Daughter Gone
Away." Contagious. On a pre-dawn jog, he touches the
silence surrounding owl hoots, thinks of lonely beings
"clinging to branches or drifting / wherever the air
moves them through the dark and cold." Delicate and
gentle. The poem epitomizes Stafford's life: he's
always sought his "place," has been "one moving voice
touching whatever is present / or might be, even what I
cannot see when it comes."

<u>Sandra</u> <u>McPherson</u> writes three tired, attitudinizing
poems, and one pretty good one. When she is bad, forced
and solipsistic, she loads in cheap pathetic fallacies,
viz., "shotguns needing ducks." She comes to life
though, in "Pornography, Nebraska." She's truckin'
along, listening to her CB unit. The voice of a dude
comes over, loud and clear, describing the tattoos on
his body, and the pain he endured having the areas
around his tit-nipples pricked. McPherson is turned on.
The voice disappears, leaving her to reflect on a man
she abandoned, recording the pain in "the bedspring
spiral" of her notebook. <u>Frederick Seidel</u>'s "The New
Cosmology" is an intelligent, tightly-executed poem,
deriving from a less than inspiring artifact--a LIFE
aerial photo of the Earth taken from space. Wouldn't
what's shown seem to God like "a naive stain of
wildflowers on a hill?" If Seidel could drop his bib-
and-tucker, and eschew pretentious adjectives ("divine
mammal," "chosen people," "almond-eyed shepherd
warriors"), he'd have a fine poem. I'm sucked into the
black hole of his abstractions. He leaves me chilled:
"The last nanosecond of silence twenty billion years ago
/ Before the big bang is endless."

<u>Naomi</u> <u>Shihab</u> <u>Nye</u>'s "The Use of Fiction" has little
to excite, nothing to condemn. <u>Stephen</u> <u>Spender</u> writes a
mannered five-part elegy, "Auden's Funeral." This
should have been moving. But it's not. Spender reviews
his days with Auden, when both were young poets; and
this section is good. But Spender strains for the
pastoral consolation. Auden is a

> ...marvellous instrument of consciousness
> With intellect like rays revealing
> Us driven out on the circumference
> Of this exploding time.

That I must be negative about such ill-felt writing,

hurts. I value the work of both poets; but, then, this elegy can't erase that.

The best poem here is by Gjertrud Schnackenberg. She writes in a traditional free-verse manner, avoiding flashy pyrotechnics. "Reading Flaubert's Letters" covers six pages. Schnackenberg reflects on Flaubert's advice to his "neglected" Louise that she read and not dream. Schnackenberg is seated before a table of books, and is exhausted from reading. The books are the towers of a city, the City of God where the spirit of Flaubert continues the quest for the perfect style. Her immediate realities? Discomfort, a cold rain on the window, the noise of the upstairs neighbors. Other motifs are brilliantly intervowen: King Lear, Pinocchio, the pentacles from the Tarot deck, a broom with a string attached (which Schnackenberg holds in her lap, like a Saint's head). She dreams, creating Flaubert's present identity.

May Swenson contributes a deceptively simple "Under the Baby Blanket." The poem, in 2-line stanzas, begins dully, with music that sounds about as subtle as beating on a pie tin with a spoon. Details: A forty-seven-year old woman returns to Swenson, bringing a baby-blanket her Mom made for her. When Swenson suggests hanging the object, as "a work of art," the former baby protests, lies down beneath the blanket, draws up her legs, and, "almost covered with little girls 47 years old," falls asleep.

I can't say much for John Hollander. His poems are bravura pieces, dazzling but shallow. The Dazzle Poem, like the Dazzle Story (as written by Updike and Cheever), and the Dazzle Art-Song (as written by Rorem), amaze with their surface brilliance. Hollander's "Hidden Rhymes," for example, entices us to poke our pink little snouts through the word-roots to ferret out all the semi-concealed rhymelets. It's fun. We feel we've snouted a fine poem. Like most Dazzle Artists, Hollander tries for Momentosity: "the heavy/ Burden of the tune we carry" hums us "to the grave." Poems like this give a magazine class, slick and ivy-smothered.

Mark Nepo, in "Oxenholme," produces a mix of prose and verse. Russell Edson is a writer I'd just about given up on; his recent work seems self-parody. Yet, he appears here with some fairly decent parables. Dave Smith winds off the U. S. poetry offerings. As usual, he mixes good writing with bad. He pretentiously relates whatever he writes to a recollected self, often in its boyhood. In itself, that's not a bad strategy. Smith, though, is too often sentimental. In a poem about Maupassant, Smith is clumsy: "As when I was a child put away by my father / in the seal of sleep." Atrocious Dylan Thomas! All the <u>yous</u> stultify, are tongue-licks spent after too much tranquility. Here, where Smith is sexual, the writing groans, like the springs of the tired bed upon which Flaubert shafts his mistress: "She took your thrust after thrust while the time /crusted in your head that would seep...." "Crusted"/"thrust" is unfortunate, and the clumsiness of the "that" construction would do justice to the worst of Matthew Arnold's spavined lines. "Snake: A Family Tale," another of Smith's recollections, is better; but, as one scrutinizes the fabric, you soon see that it's cut from the same brummagem.

In conclusion, this ANTAEUS has better work than I expected, plus much that is inept. The positives cancel the negatives. One forgives the dreck for the work by Schnackenberg and Stafford.

BOX CAR: A MAGAZINE OF THE ARTS

No. 1 (1983). Managing Editor: Paul Vangelisti. Literary Editor: Leland Hickman. PO Box 39466, Los Angeles, CA 90039. $12 for 3 issues.

This new magazine (format 8" x 11") is an ambitious mix of art work, poetry, and reviews. Leland Hickman has made his choices with a large nod towards poets puffing into reknown as The Language Poets, most of them centered in San Francisco, where they may be found sitting near Robert Duncan's sneakers at New College, or regaling one another at regular meetings of themselves where they lecture, read, and generally carry on. I understand that they now disclaim ever having been a School--yet it seems that that is exactly what they have consciously fashioned over the last half-dozen years. They've managed a pretty good press.

I propose to scrutinize this poetry, starting off with poets I find weak, moving to a few stronger ones, and, finally, treating a handful of writers only tangentially related to the others.

PART ONE

Barrett Watten behaves as if "any part" of language is "endless." If he believes that, Watten excuses himself from the normal disciplines of tropes, arguments, designs. Here is one of his worst moments-- as automatic writing it must stir old Gertie Stein in her tomb: "Equals high hurdles analogy." Even if we try to defend this as a funny little word riff, or typing exercise, spelt from a tired Sibyl's leaves, we must still wonder why it is so boring. Like many of the Language Poets, Watten likes statements that ring of the fiat or the decree: "Obscure anything that darkens." "Sound is to territory / as / Firing weapons is to talk." As for sound here, there isn't much--a good shot or two, even from a Saturday Night Special, would be welcome.

Bob Perelman's news is both esoteric and commonplace. Fortune cookies speak to strangers "on intimate terms." (Have you listened to a fortune cooky lately?) Today is different from all other days. Judgment Day occurred at birth. "We night(sic) have made a beautiful splashes of silver nitrate in some mind's eye." (That's what they drop into babies' eyes, isn't it?) "Infinite space" bounds a torchlight procession. "Language is what is told...." This last one clues us in on Perleman's running off at the mouth: as long as you keep chattering, filling up the intense inane with vocables and sibillants, the Infinitesimal Void swells like a big gas bag. Too many good lines blown in might ignite the universe. This is one of Perelman's best moments: "I am as ass and need to be kissed..." This is vaguely erotic. You may like it if you are into ass-kissing. And it's neatly grammatical. Is he "sassy?" This might be Perelman's idea: "Grammar plus person, parsed from inside, split up into ones." My ass? Your ass? Your man? My man? The trite smeared with cooky juice squiggles through the verse-sandwich--Senior-Seminar Surrealisms abound. I am looking through the hole of a record.

Yes, Carla Harryman is one of the few visible women in the movement. (Another is Lyn Hejinian). Harryman simply has more intelligence than most of the men. Her laughables (Because waves "complete the dinosaurs" there's "no possibility of starvation") are laundered through a saline mix of alphabetty (like brown betty, only cooked up with words rather than apples) as a kind of formula/recipe: a/b, c/d, g/h, etc. Things do get messy at times: "the wave reports to the doctor with a stiff upper lip." Whose lip? Does it matter? She faileth to refurbish her cliché.

As for Bruce Andrews, if you read him word for word, line for line, as I have, you may end up a zombie. Only a good five minutes of self-pinching brings you back. His rhythms are designed to accompany the March of the Living Dead. Only the dwarf who helped the golden-haired lady in the tower should be forced to pick through all this. Andrews writes a hodge-podge of one-liners Language Poets favor. Old Ralph Waldo Emerson, who couldn't have organized a paragraph if it meant he'd be spared bedding Margaret Fuller, was master of the mode. Andrews also likes imperatives. Poets who over-use them end up sounding like nagging fathers-in-law. If you try to follow their commands, you'll end up whopping your lover with a bladder full of dried peas. Here's a sample:

--Consider the poll tax, such he was pretty zealous--Sit on our hands, those spurious nail-clippers; fling down entire pop-up arm-loads--She looks like totally zombie, he d(sic) be a medical alcohol freak, tight fitting altogether stiff--Narrate out for kicks, squids a puzzle....

I am intrigued by Clark Coolidge. Many of his images are inspired (a naughty word, probably, in some

circles) both serious and funny. A looney, surreal
desert landscape appears, on which we sit, wait, and try
to be funny as we undergo our Existential Angst. At
last, we stop squeezing our ice-cream cones. Numerous
portentous moments, though, zap Coolidge: "All that has
happened is a semblance / of what could have been."
"Seems the voices / have gone back to the Other Place."
"No writing worth its salt has a point." This last
remark I like, in the sense that Poetry is not to
proseletyze, declaim, instruct. James McNeill Whistler
fought this battle in the 1890's, didn't he? and better.
So did Aubrey Beardsley. Coolidge and kind seem so
fearful of being caught with their political veins
glowing, they wax pompous, in an effort to decoy (to be
coy). John Yau's corpses aren't sufficiently fetid to
arouse much of a response in his readers--he sounds,
alas, like a re-run of Watten, Harryman, et al. But,
then, he's not well-represented here--so I may not be
fair.

One of the most admired of these poets, Charles
Bernstein, has much in common with the San Francisco
Munchkins, many of whom, like Bernstein, are expatriates
from New York City. Bernstein was co-editor, with Bruce
Andrews of the now-defunct journal L*A*N*G*U*A*G*E.
Bernstein scribbles some 60 lines crammed with
trivialities. Who cares if in "SoHo, Munich, Berlin"
there's "an international indifferance (sic)?" Is "Bob"
Bob Perelman? Cosy in-group stuff oozes forward; but, to
return to the issue of "Bob"--he can't be Duncan: he's
called Robert. Is it Creeley? "Bob" tells Bernstein:
"We screen out the / multiplicity of detail in our quest
past the / overall." I cringe, anticipating Mrs.
Murphy's chowder. No, it can't be Creeley.

When I read such neo-Platonic, neo-Fichtean, neo-
Carlylean observations, I realize that these poets are
quasi-Goethes in love with old-fashioned moon-shine
thoughts. Goethe, though, waited until he was on his
death-bed for "mehr Licht."

The oldest poet of the bunch is David Bromige,
the expatriate Britisher who has been up north for some
20 years or so. He has busied his hand at many verse
modes (Spear the Holy Kingfisher, if you must! For in
the end, we come to dust!) I like reading Bromige even
when, as here, he has little to say. He loves puns,
double-takes, and jokes: "A pretty face is like a
malady, and he was into nurses." "What a squirrel does
with his nuts, he does with their opportunities." "They
died of plague. Now all were in the same cart, not long
before the horse." Once through the fun-house what do
we find? A leech or two stuck to the groin, thinking
you are nuts.

Barbara Einzig is fond of bland abstractions. Her 12 part poem reads like scraps from a journal, written whilst meditating over some Great Book. There are spavined lines: "Transparent truth of the quiet who lean against the wall of their fatigue." Figure that one out! She likes "truth," "witnesses," drowning in water, "things going somewhere." She opines that we breathe air, "like any natives." Her nadir has to be this 3-word moment:

Language!
Your face.

Eliminate the pretentiousness, load in much self-absorption, and you have Marina La Palma. Interestingly, her paragraphs are from her "Bagatelles series." Nuff said.

The best of these writers is, I think, Ron Silliman, something of an eminence vert among these pigeons. He's probably the best theorizer in the cote. One moment here begins with a pun and proceeds to cool, subdued writing. The cadences are various--something quite lacking in the other poets. And he knows how to sustain a motif, giving us a sense that we are going somewhere, though not necessarily in a straight line. His images of squirmy earwig--bubble--drupes--goblets--squid are nicely dense, and his syntax is sufficiently fractured to satisfy the lips of your generic Language Poet. Here is the passage:

That work = word salad ballad. Regal and rusted.
Frothing, because rabid. Each day a new sky.
First the verb. A view of the lightwell. Warrior
image of earwig. I seem to be saying, I see
myself begin, I, terms bubble at their own inexact,
it it is, drupes, or goblets, space stations in
two point, ink but a trail or squid of.

Later on, he says he's after striking a balance in "this decentered freedom." That's a good way to put it--although the obvious risk is that balance may easily = boredom.

PART TWO

Now, for a look at a few poets who only tangentially, if at all, touch the Language Pen-ists. First, the managing editor himself, Paul Vangelisti. has been writing for some 10 years with qualities the

Language Poets seem to yearn for. Yet, Vangelisti's
achievements are insufficiently acknowledged--despite
the fact that he has published these poets in Invisible
City, and has consistently featured European avant-garde
writers. Perhaps if he moved to San Francisco, borrowed
Robert Duncan's cape and velvet trousers, and oraculated
before the ephebes.... But, to the point: his "GOF in
Singapore" is filled with moments that seem inspired by
gauzy, evanescent, continental films--Fitzi-Continis
Garden films...Truffaut's Jules et Jim...Antonioni mood-
scapes. His persons are glamorous, cultured, and
dessicated. They emerge from and recede into tinted
shadows, and are gentle in their regrets and liaisons.
They drift through tinted miasmas: "What she couldn't
hear was the quiet of this table.... That it's a glass
table is worth mentioning....It was literally one week
ago he had to fart and a page was missing." In this
redolent air (one imagines the fart lingering for hours
with the aromas of late apples, woodsmoke, and oiled
tennis rackets) there is mayhem--mayhem seen through
gauze. Murder brings our hero to song:

> the phone rings as the throat is cut
> the page ripped out as blood covers the hands
> and the voices approach call out names
> he tries to remember the words
> the radiant step the phone rings
> as they circle thirst like flame
> does he dare to sing

Holly Prado contributes one of the best pieces I've
seen by her; her language mirrors a caring, passionate
life. If she errs, it's when she's too loquacious.
There's a fresh dailiness here: a lover, an older woman,
meditations on physical beauty, voices in the dark.
Prado's theme is that words alone, as they reflect
feelings, keep us at a remove, if short, from the
beasts. The sequence ends this way:

> The word folds its arms around a crippled dream.
> The word does not cry.
> The word says, "There isn't much time."
> The word is awake now, at this very moment.

3 poems by Michael Palmer hover between being
mainly about grammar and about white spaces, which the
"you" (I guess it's the reader) fills in. He's sexy:
water trickles down rocks; a man observes the black
pubic fur and female parts of a urinating woman. An
injured child adds some further humanity. Palmer seems
vaguely political. See "(Overheard at the) Mayakovsky
Station." He is mildly off the wall, and is master of
his craft. I wish, though, that he weren't always so
cool, nay genteel.

Robert Kelly is up to his usual esoterica. He
contributes "Skenting" (Run to the dict., folks), an 8
part piece written on an Amtrak going up the Hudson
River Valley. He skitters brightly and even humorously,
without giving too much care to aesthetics. Like many
another of his poems (Kelly is an Arachne of Poetry),
this one too spins scintillating threads--one is
religious, the other sexual. Souls extricated from the
warp of life.

John Thomas' "From Patagonia," a work-in-progress,
is a series of short prose-poems and prose-pieces, all
lucid conjurings of a place he has never visited. When
his young son complains that Thomas seems obsessed with
Patagonia, and tells him to go there, Thomas responds,
saying he "is" in Patagonia. That sets up the frame. In
his imagined mindscape/landscape, Thomas spins us in and
out of the mundane, the trashy, and the wondrous. He
may remind readers of Frederick Prokosch of The
Asiatics. Thomas's work should be much better known
than it is. One of his books is still available from
Red Hill Press, with a longer selection from
"Patagonia" forthcoming.

Dennis Phillips' "Housenight" is an expansive love-
poem, sensitive and intense. The image of a stallion in
wet grass weaves through the central portion, as a
climax for the lovers

And the slow gallop
the slick hide
mouth of the wild night stallion
teeth extended
                    wide galloping nostrils...
the hard pounding hooves
silent in the dark but almost glowing
as they said it would be
            if all defenses were dropped....

Martha Lifson is also impressive. Her Genji poems are as
delicate as any in BOXCAR. She evokes some of the
fragility of the Japanese culture inspiring the poems.
Yet, they remain hers. Here is a fine moment:

        Her hair is as long as
the emperor's long life; when she covers her mouth
to laugh, powder comes off in her hand.

Peter Levitt is also good. Love is an image of "white on
white,.. a woman known / with my own brown hands." My
feeling is that these poems are better than some of
Levitt's more ambitious longer works. Robert Trammell,

whose work I had never seen before, writes good free-verse evocations of his childhood...sights, sounds, smells from the old house in Texas. The more ambitious poem, "The Dark Hall," could be much tighter; it tells more than it needs to. I hope Trammell reads the other poets here--he may find models for trimming his work.

Robert Crosson writes with zip and dash, almost as if he's delivering poems from the stage. (He is a professional actor). He can be as discursive as any of the language folk--but he knows how to charge his writing with emotion. He makes the reader _feel_ the need that prompted the poem. And he writes with a rampant sexual energy:

> got him on the bed, serenaded mendelssohn records
> plowed it in (his head caught under the doorsill)
> and burnt his elbows on the carpet.
>   'Shanty songs--'
> midway between a tar dock & an uptown bank of
>   cattails.
> Doubtless well-endowed...
>   Dead now of course, best friends agreed.
>   Wanted three things: to get married
>   make a baby and commit suicide.
> Wrote haiku, fucked and exploded.

And this is so fresh, so right: "I am my car, I am my Christmas pajamas." If there is one line in this magazine I want to remember, this is it! His "Home Letters. A Vaguely Ontological Aspiration" is a collage tour-de-force. Is he having his fun at the expense of the Language Poets? He juxtaposes passages from humdrum found letters ("They never heard from Ron since he left the east") with aesthetical statements probably shaped in discussions with Paul Vangelisti and the Italian avant-garde poet Adriano Spatola. When he asks the serious, final question about his own work, he juxtaposes a "letter from home" which ends on the trivial, and with a laugh. The laugh counts. Here are the two passages:

> Is my work, in its refusal of the
>
> dichotomy, political engagement/
>
> disengagement, a poetry based on
>
> vaguely ontological aspirations?
>
> And in its refusal of silence,
>
> does it hide perhaps a pseudo

<u>demiurgical</u> <u>need</u> <u>to</u> <u>render</u> <u>the</u>

<u>word</u> <u>sacred?</u>

Don't know full particulars.   Ed's
working at Riverside gets
most every day in. Grace
got your card said she had
a good laugh about it. &
tell you thanks.

So, BOXCAR #1. Despite the wasted space devoted to
Bay Area poets, the mix is valuable. There's nil
Academic Sleaze, nil Stodge. The editors, Hickman in
particular, deserve credit for publishing what seems a
new trend in American verse. It's not their fault that
this much-hyped stuff isn't better than it is. Reading
literary magazines is akin to reading TIME or NEWSWEEK
or THE ATLANTIC MONTHLY--some things grab you, and
others don't. My guess is that BOXCAR will improve as it
goes along--printing less but better poetry and more
art. The concept behind the journal is fresh.

CHELSEA

No. 40(1981). Editor: Sonia Raiziss. PO Box 5880. Grand Central Station, New York, NY 10163. $7 for two issues.

CHELSEA is a magazine poets seem to send their best work to. Much credit belongs to Sonia Raiziss and to her editorial staff. They seem to wait for a body of good stuff before they publish. There are over two dozen poets in this issue.

William Joyce writes a long poem on still-birth and death, one drenched in trauma, blood, and pain, universalized via allusions to fairy-tales. He writes accessibly, with sharp details, scalpel-clean. Here's a passage:

Her mother was stretched across a mountain
Bulging up through her spine
Where the wind whistled like knives.
The child was her mother, tumbling down
Each corridor like rain.
A brother was being born
But the mountain was giving birth
To boulders rumbling in the wake
Of bodies on rubber wheels
Rounding each corridor.

Deborah Pease employs reportage (and we and you) to reflect her frustrations. The furnace isn't working. A crayfish behind a tiny aquarium castle is dying. The poet sits in view of the Empire State Building--"a mighty symbol at this distance / But tawdry up close." It's cold. She's tired. Pease's plainness and simplicity are powerful; she doesn't need fancy, pompous phrasings.

Helped by God, Sarah White "creates Eve on a Prayer-Book Page," and then translates herself and her Adam to condos where they are doomed to birthing babies. Adam suffers without tenure. Paradise is

...a place they used to play, a place
Like a tapestry. One thread hung
From a knot of figs, shining.

She tugged it, for the fun,
And saw a whole garden come undone.

29

Jordan Smith fashions six free-verse sonnets
inspired by Edvard Munch. Three are fine. Smith begins
well, devoting the opening quatrains to evocations of
Munch. One poem concludes this way: "For what can't
change or last: a still figure / and the bridge already
rushing toward the margin." Here is a syphilitic child:

A child blossoms with sores because his father
couldn't keep his fly zipped, and the mother,
an open sore herself, cradles him in the doctor's
suite in her bloodshot dress. . . .

This is good, and Smith relates these ironies to his own
life--a cow skull in a woods, a woman crying because her
baby is backwards in her womb, a father emerging from
shock treatment.

John Tagliabue shows that he can write more than
skinny poems. Paul Hoover humorously evokes a male
model in a life-class who won't stop talking. Stephen
Bett's "Preparation for a Gift" is an Ashbery-like
disquisition on Jackson Pollock splattering those
canvases. Jody Swilky's imitation of Vallejo turns on
frayed images of slums, dark, streets and scary
footsteps. Bill Sylvester contributes a long, stodgy
piece on drying, collecting, and using herbs. There's a
dulling monotony, and like many "poems" adapted from
prose-books, the effects weary. More is less, I fear.

David Lunde mixes in awful clichés: "inexpressible
joy," "my heart pulses like a star." Robert Billings is
on track. In "Song of the Open Eyes" he takes a trite
topic--the"bird poem." But he doesn't tell that we are
in for a grisly rollercoaster carnage-ride. Birds and
worms strip skin from men. Birds gobble worms. "Just
After Dark" features two cats too dumb to wear those new
flea collars that glow. As they claw the headlights,
they are smeared.

The slaphappy dissection
With cleavers sharp branches

Eyes jabbed against the skull
stomach chopped to the spine

The illustration has blood spattered on trees
the usual full moon
seven ratty broomsticks

The dervish of crotch hair
deformed limbs

tells the joy of all this

John Brandi should be better; he's still writing from a counter-culture life begun in the late 50's and continuing through India, Central America, and the American Southwest. The impact of his style (and the poem runs for three pages) is trivial and predictable:

Cranes disassembling into alphabet glitter
above my son who whistles his way
to third grade, past thousand-year-old petroglyphs.
Maya pulls the tongue from her shoe.

Robert Bonazzi is "learning," he informs us, to live with stones in his mouth. W. M. Aberg is better. His prose poem says that we hate being told we're like everybody else, especially when we're having our portrait drawn. And in "The Listening Chamber" he creates an effectively deadened voice reminiscent of Magritte. His theme, though, seems a bit hokey. If we haven't done some things in life we're "afraid of being caught for," we haven't lived.

Amy Clampitt signs in with a poem on a New York shopping-bag lady. Her lavish details enrich a moving narrative design. Carol Cavallaro writes of another old woman who sees herself as "a nun...cold / and intellectual." She finds blood everywhere. Her sink is stuffed with a sweater, but the sink keeps gurgling, "infantile." She imagines herself flying about the country in a snowy wind. Later, she freezes her body to an aluminum door-frame. Poignant. Katherine Kane expects Mr. Right to turn up, a man so "overheated" he'll bite into your veins. He never shows.

Two boring poems by Jarold Ramsey. A better one, on the pointlessness of "Modern" as a style, by Tom Disch. Mary Ruefle writes The Academic Abroad Poem. She visits Ghent Cathedral and freshly observes the effigies of Charles the Bold and his daughter Mary. David Wagoner is livelier than usual. Stephen Dunn's "Silence" fails to transcend the sentimental soothing of a child; he sits on a porch waiting for the moon. Roberta Metz proves to her son that he's hers by pointing to the same birthmark on her thigh that's on his. In "Witness" she frees a parrot who then helps the police arrest her by screaming: "You did." Two narcissistic poems by Florence Grossman who tortures a cat. Martha King's "Ailanthus Songs" eulogizes a stink tree "married to cat piss / in dank backyards." Much stench and sneezing. Facts about the tree are gleaned, it seems, from a botany book--the tree has a mixed sexuality. Rarely do poets invest a set-piece with this much originality.

Cheers for CHELSEA 40.

CHICAGO REVIEW

Vol. 33: no. 1(Summer 1981). Editors: Molly McQuade and John L. Sutton. University of Chicago, 5700 S. Ingleside, Box C, Chicago, IL 60637. $10 per year.

Nature pink, rather than red, in tooth and claw dominates most of this work. There is much bucolicism. A turtle drags her "carapace" from the sea and deposits eggs in a moon-drenched landscape. A boy initials the soft tar of a one-lane country road. A man, wife, and babe confront life in a forest. One feels secure with such topics--so many poets have written them. Many academics, dear John Muir, since they derive from farms and hamlets, like these sentimental returns and regurgitations.

When Laurence Lieberman worms through Boulder Caves we perk up, expecting a speleology of life, leading to hairy, fresh speculations. But they don't happen; and the comfort-inducing iambs turn trivial. Lieberman's bloke slums through nature, unable to follow the authentic spelunkers who leave three sets of sneakers (Father, Son and Holy Ghost?) behind: small shoe-prints in the Adidas-sands of Time! I listen for the mail at the front door.

In "Some Nights" Elton Glaser's tongue belabors itself questing for metaphors. Our lives are as boring as Kansas. Brian Swann does better with "Pig Moon, Turtle Moon"--once past the opening fashioned in the Gary Snyder Ugh Manner. (I might note that Swann is a good chameleon poet--he can write like nearly anybody he sets his mind to--no small gift). Here he does Snyderesque Primitive Talk, and eschews the full-blown verse line:

> The moon's horns stick
> into sky's wall.
> Shine like a tusk.
> Pig moon. Moon

Shortly, though, a moon-struck loggerhead turtle appears, depositing "germs of life."

Turner Cassity would like to appear primitive, but
merely produces hunks of suet: "kinds of airlessness,"
"a cold monotony," "many-lettered /Tetragammaton,"
"warm oasis," and "scarred patricide of Time." He
means, I think, to write an Adam coming-into-
consciousness poem. He's so dully Shakespearean, his
jawbreakers add up to little. He loves the lumbering
iamb, viz.:

                                    In blue
    Air changed as wind and brightened for our sky
    That still, that dark we share is tempered.
Answers...

Timothy Steele fashions a pair of throw-back poems
via forced verbs. Sentimentality sticks to the poem
like crystalline gums on a spruce tree. A boy chews
"the sweetness from long stalks of grass." A babe in a
cradle, complete with frontier parents, can't "guess the
storm will end / Or that in time he will be led /To the
mad variousness of hope." Ugh.

Terry Stokes was worth waiting for: your daughter
comes in late the first night after she removes her
"thousand dollar braces." This "suddenly perfect,"
protected teen-ager displays "love bites" all over her
neck. Stokes is crisp and funny-- no fancy metaphysics
or defunct literary echoes.

FIELD

No. 25 (Fall 1981). Editors: Stuart Friebert and David
Young. Oberlin, OH 44074. $6 per year.

FIELD lies very fallow indeed, thoroughly low-
keyed. All's right in the poetry world, FIELD seems to
say: lakes stand unruffled, the minor mode prevails, and
old values represented by old poets (Rilke), by the

sweet faces of dead relatives, and by scenes of rural life (complete with untilled fields) dominate verse. Sound casual, experiential, write passably, and fill your rifts with mundane notes from the kitchen stoops and environs. Reading through FIELD, we sense a need for much more energy afoot and afield.

Poems and interviews in homage to Robert Francis on his eightieth birthday start things off. Francis emerges as a very minor Robert Frost. He has a gentle / genteel Thoreauvian wisdom, with ironies so quiet they won't press many of the wrinkles out of your ethics-birthday suits or raise more than a dainty chigger bite on your arm. A couplet from one of Francis's poems sums it up, a commentary on the poems in FIELD: "The stones are gray / and so are they."

One of the editors, David Young, poles backwards along life's poetry stream with yet another translation of Rilke. The other editor, Stuart Friebert, translates Ilse Aichinger who recollects that she walked into icy water without her shoes, and that both her calves "were driven to slaughter." If an American poet had written that, a butcher would have slit her throat without that coup de grace all animals about to be slaughtered deserve--a blow to the skull. Perhaps the editors of magazines should publish their works in magazines they don't edit.

Brenda Hillman is cute before she descends to pomposity and truism: "Another year gets up / and walks away." "My car is small and slow / like marriage...." "I know / what safety comes from wanting nothing." Russell Edson messes around with three slight fables. J. E. Polster locates her grandmother's eyes in an old puppet. Scary. Michael Harper slackly commemorates an old black woman who ran the kitchen at Yaddo for years; she was an artist in cloth and thread (bread). Dennis Schmitz writes of the old folks in what I call the Colostomy Bag Poem: Uncle Lucien stank. But so did life. Old grandma, with stiffening fingers, created a tree-of-heaven quilt, placing her own fetal image between her parents' shapes. She waited tidily beneath her Oxydol-iridescent sheets for Death.

FIELD is a thin, closed show. The editors are utterly conservative. The poems by William Stafford closing the magazine hit the note: laid-back, reflective, seemingly trivial. Be advised: you know the poem you'll have to write if you want to appear here. Haunt your past a little, be prosaic, choose home-baked subjects, and whip them off in low, low keys.

THE GEORGIA REVIEW

Vol. XXXVI: No. 1 (Spring 1982). Editor: Stanley W. Lindberg. University of Georgia, Athens, GA 30602. $6 per year.

Thirty-six years of poetry, reviews, and stories have flashed beneath the magnolias! After all this time, you might expect some Southern Stodge. THE GEORGIA REVIEW looks inviting and tasteful--white and blue cover with photo of Dana Andrews and Anne Baxter consulting with Jean Renoir, during the filming of Swamp Water (1941). The issue is fat (232pp. excluding ads), and at less than two dollars per copy has to be one of the best magazine bargains in the U. S. A.

An uninspired poem by William Logan leads off. "Dream Contract" is a workshop poem, written with no evidence of heart-blood. Logan, repetitious, likes rhetorical flourishes ("will not trade season," "the fetters...are incorruptible"). Jared Carter offers "Digging," another failed Self-Assignment Poem in which a poet takes what seems an arbitrary topic and develops it. Carter likes the "darkness" tag. Up goes Existentialism, along with some easy observations and spavined cadences:

> Somebody invented a machine to dig graves.
> It would dig ditches, too. Now, if you think
>
> Of the earth as a book, there are pages missing,
> Passages no one turns to anymore.

Mary Oliver's Self-Assignment Poem is a bit better, despite the fact that via "Skunk Cabbage" she provides a genteel reminder of your roots in

> ...the woods you love,
> where the secret name
> of every death is life again--a miracle
> wrought surely not of mere turning
> but of dense and scalding reenactment.

She knows that life isn't always rendered in Technicolor: "What blazes the trail is not necessarily pretty."

Franz Douskey whittles an enormous idea ("History of Night") down to pigmy size via talked rather than felt moments, and a monotonous scattering of dull, polysyllabic adjectives: "a complete mystery," "a tidal wave of darkness," "animal fidelity" "inverted nights," "cobwebbed memory," "sudden leap." Edward Hirsch, in his "Night" poem ("The Night Parade"), could use some Swiftian bite. Despite bravura writing, especially in the final stanza, this is yet another example of Poetry Stodge. Stan Sanvel Rubin's "Last Day of February" is unpretentious and brief; he's carried away questing after similes. But the poem is soon over.

The best poem here is David Ray's "Richard St. George, Esquire, Orders His Portrait from Henry Fuseli, 1791." Archaic touches convince us that St. George, not Ray, does the talking. Furthermore, the character poignantly strives to keep a likeness of himself for his descendants--he knows he is dying. And he asks Fuseli, the great painter of nightmares, to render him old, "grown haggard, with melancholy Madness." His children will see the image "as if from God, a miracle beheld." He further instructs Fuseli:

> You should paint me if you can when you too
> have been told the fatal symptoms--three weeks
> after a doctor's word would catch it best.

Certainly, the poem owes something to Robert Browning-- here too a life is in crisis. Ray's poem has vigor and panache. He shakes the old magnolia tree, and is unabashedly old-fashioned as he does so.

L. L. Zeiger displays phlegm strangling on a "small piece of itself." John Frederick Nims, a.k.a as the editor of POETRY, writes in the manner of Joyce and Berryman, winding off with an old concept reminiscent of Dante Gabriel Rossetti's House of Life: a "soul in a soul" spinning around the North Pole, with Space and Time. Some readers will find the old-fashioned, almost Elizabethan turn of this passage fun:

> Lay your head closer, love. It's world on world
> When lips on, up, in, under lips are curled.

With Robert Farnsworth, Coleman Barks, Peter Cooley, and Charles Fort we return to well-trodden ground. Fort loves the pathetic fallacy: a landscape that "fails you, divides you," and a moon that lays its "scribble on the pond." He is also enamored of Alliteration Sleaze:

> ...how your own
> proud heart might someday come to painful
> poise...

Barks reaches for the universal (he writes well). A voice urges us to recall our origins. We carry "stuff" from our past, "machines and tires and pieces of iron." In "the flowing river," others are with us: "we accidentally brush against each other sometimes." Cooley, daughters in hand, goes out to watch darkness settle, hoping that his siblings will recall gazing across that river, and sharing a "shadowless," "starless" life. Fort sneaks in sentimental touches; his poem seems stronger than it is--"marching men" rule "something called a city." This symbol matters: "the form of a child / with spiked fists and golden arms" lifting "a bird by its bright wing."

So much for the verse. Little invites a second glance. If magnolia trees were used for pulp, what a waste of fibers! All of the poetry reviewed (by conservative Peter Stitt, a featured reviewer) is published by trade or university presses, and are raved over: Random House (twice), University of Georgia Press (twice), Wesleyan University Press. Do Stitt and his ilk pay any attention whatsoever to publishers other than the pillared Taras of Poetry?

THE HUDSON REVIEW

Vol. XXXIV: Nos.3 & 4(1981,1982). Editors: Paula Deitz and Frederick Morgan. 65 East 55th St., New York, NY 10022. $12 per year.

The audience for THE HUDSON REVIEW is clearly not the audience for THE WORMWOOD REVIEW, LITTLE CAESAR, BARNEY, NAUSEA, or CARNAL ABUSE. Nor do the host of followers who jam readings by Bukowski, Ginsberg, Rich, and Snyder, followers who don't read books, care whether the HUDSON REVIEW exists or not. In fact, most of these people wouldn't have heard of it. The world of American poetry is fractured. One shouldn't fault a journal as old as this one for appealing to audiences who like facile verse. A bilious melancholy must be gently induced.

Dana Gioia opens with poems on composers and musicians: Pachmann, Bach, Bruckner, and Haydn. (Gioia might read Charles Bukowski's poem on Borodin to see how a real master writes on these themes). There are depressing views of a rich kid in a city apartment on a rainy afternoon. Lucille Day introduces us to Tomboy Karen who ends up stabbed 87 times; a fancy-woman sitting in a welfare office; and a neurochemist who's about to slash off mice-heads in the interests of brain research. Day has guts. The weakest poet is Alicia Ostriker. "The Pure Unknown" is drenched in Academic Sleaze. Phrases clunk like the chains of the Ghost of Christmas Past: "the immeasureable feel," "the system of the world," "the virtue of the pure unknown." And the self-display of the good books she's read (LEAR, CRIME AND PUNISHMENT, and Thomas Aquinas) doesn't evoke the purity she desires. Her terza rima is no mean feat, though she shaves on the rhymes: keen doesn't quite fit with passion.

There's a very mixed performance by Richard Cole. A terrific "Recovering in the Sandwich Islands" is followed, alas, by a sterile "Aubade," the latter not the sort of morning song anybody would rise to. Kathryn Stripling's dad drops dead while urinating (she actually says "piss"). Alison Turner's "Cobble Hill," a narrative poem, deals with a woman pursuing a mate who misses the trail. Turner provides what might be an epigram for this entire GUIDE: "That day there were too many words."

One of the editors, Frederick Morgan, dominates the winter issue. While his five poems make you work, his forms are very derivative. though competent. One of his persons says: "I work a slick witchcraft that joins to beauty." That's truer than he, the poet, wots. The best of Morgan's poems, "The Reflection," approaches a mad vision spoiled by lumbering words and phrases:

--Clothe me in jaguar skin, give me secret wings
to ride the difficult air of this sardonic vision
that enunciates a night-sky to a million aching tribes--
but do not ask me, like a luckier man, to propound....

"The difficult air" is leaden. "Sardonic" is editorializing. The "that" bridging lines 2 and 3 is clumsy. "To propound" recalls old Robert Browning confused in his verse-web.

Jean Nordhaus's poems are refreshing. She writes forcefully of the death of a mother. A poem to her father is also moving.

Like most of these periodicals, HUDSON REVIEW sticks to reviewing trade or university press books. Dana Gioia, in "Poetry Chronicle," reviews books dropped by the Louisiana State University Press, Oxford University Press, Faber and Faber, Viking, University of Illinois Press, Ohio University Press, and George Braziller. Only because he reviews the Ohio edition of

Janet Lewis' POEMS OLD AND NEW, does Gioia examine Symposium Press and Matrix Press, two obscure publishers of Lewis. Robert Phillips, contributor of another "Poetry Chronicle," slavers over these presses: Knopf, Macmillan, Atheneum, Carnegie-Mellon, Johns Hopkins, University of Missouri, Cleveland State, Norton, Louisiana State, University of Illinois. Enough said!

THE IOWA REVIEW

Vol. XI: No. 2/3(Spring-Summer 1980).   Poetry Editor:
Marvin Bell. University of Iowa, Iowa City, IA 52242.
N.p.

The editors tout THE IOWA REVIEW as "part of the
grassroots of contemporary American literature." They
are, they boast, "intent on showing that something
fresh, artful, and intelligent, something with a chance
to endure can be discovered continually." A modest aim.
One has an image of squirming wormbits and pieces of
vegetable growth rampant beneath the soil of American
literature, avidly consuming corpses and thrusting forth
as thistles, asters, sunflowers, mulleins, and timothy
strands. I'm suspicious of this agrarian image. The
American Gothic poetry-folk of Iowa City plump our
verse-granaries with wheat, rye, and soybeans. A good-
grain wholeness Ewell Gibbons would rattle his spoon
for.

Well, what is this heartland poetry like, as it
writhes juicy roots through the fat fat pages (304) of
this issue? I count 43 poems, a generous spread indeed,
even for a double issue. Most poems are written by
poets who are either at Iowa or who have been there. One
should not be surprised to find a dull sameness, an
obsession with plain facts rendered in the first person,
a penchant for trivia bordering on the hackneyed, and a
tatting of forms in the pattern of those old wedding-
ring quilts grandma made.

Rather than remain general, let me illustrate.
Stephen Berg (of ABR notoriety) tells us that "it rained
last night." He walks to his office, as "life quietly
itself" is "quietly passing." He recalls peeping up the
dress of a fat woman on a doorstoop who spread her sour
crotch: "secret preparations through the black crack."
Berg didn't gaze "directly," he wants us to believe.
Now, downtown, he stares at "beds of tulips everywhere."
He doesn't know what he "felt about her thing! / It's
casual, outdoor presence defined it as ordinary."

Thomas Swiss spreads first person phrases with
abandon, potato sprouts gone mad in a dank root cellar:
"I had the heater / turned on." "I was thinking / Of
physical comfort." "I verged on understanding." "I feel
a measure of guilt." You may prefer to see Swiss's
poems as cheese: the absolutes are the holes in them.
Judith Moffett supplies us with the ubiquitous

cancer poem. Here an old lady, a "brittle tree of a woman," contracts it. <u>David Schloss</u> writes about small dreams. He pushes a pin (his <u>pin-is</u>?) into the world he knows so little of. In "City of Angels," he hangs around his living room "to the point of dullness, dryness." (I didn't say that, folks; Schloss did).

Great! A good poem, finally. And it's about plants and growth, earth-stuff: "Green Thumb." <u>Diane Wakoski</u> wrote it. She swings her pruning hook through the heartland with the prowess of Mother Time with a scythe. She gives us jungles, crawling Gardens of Eden "where one might have to sin / just in order to come out of the brambles." Alas, surcease is brief: <u>Stanley Plumly</u> returns us to the vapid via "flowers along the railway or the river, / poorer with every passage." Here are creatures we should pity: a bird flying into a window-pane, a dog tied up in the yard, dumb folk who "talk only to themselves." <u>Dennis Schmitz</u> writes of "peripheral animals," squirrels and pheasants in the burdock. He also commemorates a hunter's wife in these wonderfully stark terms:

> she follows the puckered skin with a match
> to burn off pin feathers,
> pushes & kneads squirrels from their hides,
> printing against a haunch,
> against the suddenly revealed
> scraped breastbone, her live flesh.
> the knife-knick will be cooked in--
> even the trash organs. . . .

Schmitz is inventive--cuts (yes, the pun is intended) above most of the other poets here. Real heartland writhing, life with its clots, red and shivering.

<u>Sharon Bryan</u> tells of a daughter she might have had, something <u>Weldon Kees</u> did much better. To her, imagined children are "constant companions." Three poems by <u>William Stafford</u> follow. The best is "Remembering Brother Bob." <u>David Ray</u> visits Pompeii and blends past and present: the painted sun above the smog evokes the old volcano: "Again the trees / lie down like hair upon a head." <u>Jane Miller</u> wallows in abstractions. Her grassroots don't produce many blades--too many words like <u>knowledge, beauty, secrets, sleep, time</u>, and <u>idea</u> poison her poem-scape.

<u>Debra Gregor</u> sits in her parlor embroidering the "difference between novels and life." Oh, dear, she's left the laundry on the line. <u>Mary Jane White</u> is scatalogical: she visits the outhouse, sits on "the carpeted seat" and craps. She is moved (embowelled?). A skunk or a coon scares "the shit" out of her. Her poem

is a needed, if noisome, whiff of air. In her next poem,
commemorating Iowa flatness, boring first-person phrases
sit like sick ducks. William Logan writes tediously of
a natural setting. He can't eschew clinkers of sound:
"feeling diminished," "the moment of recognition," "the
dull procession," "a meeting of possibility."

After a strong prose-poem by Robert Bly, we return
to bathos. Daniel Halpern's five-part "Elegies for
Careless Love" is facile. His dude, one suspects,
copulated only in the missionary position. He seemed
more enamored of the moonlight striking his shoulder
than of the girl. Then he complains of old women "on
geritol." Was his friend a geriatric case? These elegies
rock placidly while rain "fingers" the wooden shingles:

> We went into the other room
> and i was the end of nothing,
> or not of anything that had started.

On New Year's Eve, 1979, Charles Wright wallows in the
solipsism we have come to expect from him:

> Will Charles look on happiness in this life?
> Will the past be the present ever again?
> Will the dead abandon their burdens and walk to the
>   river bank?

He saves himself by identifying with some hermit crabs
on the beach, brainy little crustaceans all:

> What matters to them is what comes up from below,
>   and from out here
> In the deep water,
>   and where the deep water comes from.

Jorie Graham's snake laps up butterflies and becomes an
image of us: each of our deaths is a stitching of the
earth, a "going / back under," and a "coming back up."
She does run on, winding down with desire and passion,
poisonous abstractions her garden needeth not. Workshop
stuff.

O, Iowa Review!

KAYAK

#59 (June 1982). Editors: George Hitchcock and Marjorie Simon. 325 Ocean View Avenue, Santa Cruz, CA 95062. $5 per year.

After nearly sixty issues, KAYAK remains one of the most readable of our literary magazines. You may be irritated or bored, but you won't find Academic Sleaze. And the magazine is crammed. There are some 70 pages of poetry, featuring some 35 poets. George Hitchcock, the indefatigable editor and adult-terrible, is known for his fondness for Surrealism. KAYAK, though, is not ossified into a single mode. You'll find a number of regulars: Mezey, McDowell, Lappin, Simic, Finkel, Morris, Magowan. You will also find many new voices. In fact, the best poems in this issue are by new poets. Let me mark some of the best work.

Jack Driscoll is an original. His "playing piano at the oldfolks home" is a stark, simply-written jab in the groin. A son plays for his crippled folks. The father stands "drunk without his cane," while the mother motors over in a "silver wheelchair." A second poem, "there are reasons to lie," concludes with a stunning image of blind twins going to an eye bank. What they can't see is that the bank is in flames. Mary Ann McFadden swings through commonplace events with feeling. Here three men with a tar machine lay a roof:

> I like the way the redneck dances
> smoothing the tarpaper flat
> and the way the Greek slathers the tar--hot,
> slick as butter on his bread.

Kathleen Spivack's "the peregrine" is a paradigm of a woman trapped by a lover who treats her as a falconer would treat his hawk. It's frightening--for she can't break away. He covers her eyes with a black leather glove, hoods "the fierce questions," and bandages her mind.

Robert McDowell's "put your hand up to the tv and touch mine" is nicely cryptic. The speaker owns a comatose child, an empty icebox, and a dead mother. What's the mother up to? Busy asphyxiating herself in the garage. There's a twist at the end: "I love you but I've got to go. / I'm healed and mighty sleepy." Nancy Willard, one of our older pros, takes sports headlines and writes good poems with Biblical overtones. "Tigers,

Birds Trade Pitchers" provides her with a short history
of the development of carnage on this planet. These may
be tours de force, but they are fraught with
originality. And the mysterious Herbert Morris (he
publishes almost exclusively with KAYAK) scores again
with "lost," a meditation over photos of young soldiers
that turn up in his mail:

> Light pours here, pours, but pours to no avail.
> Those standing out in it, you feel, are drenched
> beyond endurance by the time they come in,
> if, in fact, they come in. Time has the look
> of what one knows cannot quite be retrieved.

We need a book by Morris. I urge some aficionado to
glean his work from past KAYAKS and publish them.

Robin Magowan writes a five-part "while falling
asleep." It won't put you to sleep. David St. John is
vivid. His "jade" presents a carved warrior, "white as
mutton fat," with sword raised against "some injustice
or betrayal." Hadassah Stein contributes an elegy on
Archbishop Romero assissinated in San Salvador.

Now, for some carpings. The better-known poets are
the weak ones. Donald Finkel rides with his sweetie
from Indiana to Wheeling, and equates writing verse with
being trapped inside the transmission of an auto. Tom
McKeown's verses sound like parodies of Surrealist
poems: "I have clamshells for ears." There's "an
octopus wheelchair filled / with apricots." Judith
Berke is self-conscious: "I could start this with a
child / in Venice." Most disappointing are five poems
by Charles Simic. He writes here with small
distinction, and parodies his own better work. In
"ancestry," his best poem, Simic interrupts an
executioner who runs after a ball of yarn an ancient
ancestor, spectator at the beheading, dropped:

> One imagines the hooded executioner
> And his pasty-faced victim
> Interrupting their grim business
> To come smiling to their aid
>
> Confirmed pessimists
> And other party-poopers
> Categorically reject
> Such far-fetched notions
> Of gallows equiquette

Robert Mezey sets an owl in a tree and spews dull mouth-
breakers at it: "our speechless dreams," "fading into
false dawn," "full of foreboding."
Heather McHugh, queen of the Writing Conference

Circuit, contributes four flashy poems, word riffs. She makes us want to wash her mouth out with soap for not being more outrageous. McHugh pickaxes an accustomed vein. The numerous students she regales in workshops will feel titillated but won't find fresh adits to explore. So with Linda Lappin: she likes those you poems, where the you seems phony, an archetypal non-person, cardboard. Finally, Robert Peterson contributes a pair of Whiffenpoofian pieces--very casual, relaxed, even when he's telling us about scattering his Aunt Althea's ashes.

What does all this mean? KAYAK is alive. The complaints one hears that it has outlived its pizazz simply are not true. Over half this issue excites me, and for poetry mags these days that's a record.

THE KENYON REVIEW

New Series Vol.IV: No.1 (Winter 1982). Editors: Ronald Sharp and Frederick Turner. Kenyon College, Gambier, OH 43022. $5 per year.

In rating literary magazines as one does motels, KENYON would appear on all the Recommended Lists--clean, spacious, swag-lamped, with sanitized toilet seats complete with strips of ambassadorial paper over the bowls. Moderately affluent travellers will feel right at home in this three-star accommodation. Turner et al. name their suites after celebrities, viz., The James Dickey Suite, The Galway Kinnell Suite, etc. They don't goof around much with lesser figures.

Ja̲m̲e̲s̲ D̲i̲c̲k̲e̲y̲ leads off with six poems,
celebrations of a "Deborah" who visits him in the
winter of his life and revs his lust. I find all of
these poems but one ("Doorstep, Lightning, Waif-
Dreaming") embarrassing. The occasional fresh moment
("heron-veins over the forest") can't save the forced,
clotted writing. The first, "Deborah in Mountain
Sounds: Bell, Glacier, Rose," never transcends the
cloying compound adjectives or the hisses. As Dickey
strokes his aging body, a poem comes into full glans
bloom. His thrust at Deborah is "the glacier's rammed
carry / Of upheaval." And his penis (so I read the
passage), "inch-dreaming under the oval // Of the bell
interruptedly cloven," results finally in "the making-
fluid of men." In "Ray-Flower," Deborah is a "winged
seed." Dickey's poems reflect what I have elsewhere
called "tortoise writing." (In "James Dickey," THE
GREAT AMERICAN POETRY BAKE-OFF: SECOND SERIES,
Scarecrow Press, 1982). He deposits a compound word or
a clumsy phrase, then, like a weary tortoise, pauses as
the creature rests, producing a white space.
Eventually, Dickey recaptures some old magic, which he
soon spoils by awkward phrasings: "the psychic mob-
sound of bees." I am let down. When the old fire
blazes, however, Dickey is still amazing:

                    ...I come of a root-system of fire, as it
          fires
Point-blank at this hearthstone and doorstep: there is
               A tingling of light-sensitive hairs
               Between me: my clothes flicker
And glow with it, under the bracketing split
Of sky, the fasting, saint-hinting glimmer,
     The shifting blasts of echo, relocating,
          And of an orphaning blaze

     A trio of poems by J̲a̲m̲e̲s̲ M̲o̲o̲r̲e̲ easy, casual, and
slack, oscillate around platitudes. As Moore ages, he
is pulled towards a sea of death. The sky reflects his
face and seems "a close friend." His birthday is the
occasion for being lazy. Friends bearing gifts are
"patient" with his dozing, "with the punchy sleep of the
one still digesting rib eye, / with their friend who
lags--as usual--just a little behind the voices / he
loves...." He's laid-back, and thoroughly forgettable.
M̲a̲r̲g̲a̲r̲e̲t̲ B̲e̲n̲b̲o̲w̲,̲ on the other hand, is good. Her tale of
emerging from scarlet fever is taut and celebratory. Her
"Burlesque Night at Le Cave" focuses with ardor on two
trashy burlesque queens. B̲r̲a̲d̲ L̲e̲i̲t̲h̲a̲u̲s̲e̲r̲ writes so
casually of a complacent surburbanite killed in an
accident, he almost dissuades us from reading the poem.

     G̲a̲l̲w̲a̲y̲ K̲i̲n̲n̲e̲l̲l̲ has lost nary a whit of his mastery.
One poem commemorates the death of seven people riding

in an octoped. His style is crammed with interlocked
half and cross rhymes, drenched in a marvellous light.
His "Ghost Train," charred and laden with ashes,

> must merely wander into the natural world
> where all are born, where all suffer, where many
> scream,
> where the lost are not healed but gathered and used
> again.

The second poem, "Coinaliste," is a joy. It's randy,
turning as it does on these puns--<u>cunt-a-liste</u> and
<u>cunnilingus.</u> The heroine is one of those legendary
women in a trashy bar who retrieves money with her
labia.

   <u>Amy Clampitt's</u> "Triptych" disappointed me greatly
at first, despite the maggots flaying the wildebeest,
choirboys trampling entrails, and the capture of a
"fuzzed runt" by a cheetah. She employs an old
rhetoric, vaguely Shakespearean, which I associate with
bad poems written by women (often by those using three
names). In the first poem, "Palm Sunday," sets up this
complaint:

> Neither the wild tulip, poignant
> and sanguinary, nor the dandelion
> blowsily unbuttoning, answers
> the gardener's imperative, if need be....

Maiming and hampering are part of the bestial order. A
long poem, "Good Friday," constitutes itself around the
imperative "Think of...." We are asked to think of
Serengeti lions, red-necked vultures, the cheetah,
Charles Darwin, and Good Friday. Clampitt, finally,
does pull me in. She concludes with twenty-five vivid
lines, all bloody from the kill. She uses effective
Shakespearean touches; viz., "the evolving ordonnance of
murder."

LITTLE CAESAR

Vol. VII(Spring 1983). Editor: Dennis Cooper. % Beyond Baroque, 681 Venice Blvd., Venice, CA 90291. $5 per year.

Choose one, Los Angeles or New York. Boys or girls. Cherries or kumquats. Look no further--you'll find them all here in this latest LITTLE CAESAR, the most ambitious of all numbers of this irregularly appearing magazine to date. Cooper has selected a smorgie of writers balanced evenly between Los Angeles and New York. The initial piece, "A Californian Comes to New York and Finds There is No Place to Jog in the Ghetto," by Chuck Krenzin, is a juicy kiss planted on the navel of Los Angeles. Slowly, New York emerges, by comparison, defacatory, urinary, spermicidal, loaded. Numerous excellent photos, drawings, and collages are scattered throughout, by Sherree Levin, Judith Spiegel, Tom Clark, and Henry Dewitt. Featured is young New York performance artist Tim Miller, complete with numerous good photos (in the cover shot he is naked to the waist and has his name sprayed with black Rustoleum on his chest) and samples of his poetry.

THE POEMS

Michael Brownstein writes a long poem and prosy pieces in a New York soap-opera vein. He means to educate, and lets us know he's restless:

> People love each other
> desperately
> but they hate
> everyone else calmly.

Yet, there's a "White Goddess" who'll bring chicken soup as America dies. Brownstein isn't ready to throw in his personal towel though: his lover's navel still drives him crazy, and he's being sued for divorce. Were things better in 1960, when you could be a "bohemian in a t-shirt" and live on next to nothing? Alas, things have changed: these are the days of tit clips and masochism. Endless sleeping, eating, kissing, and screwing. So, deaden the mind.

Douglas Messerli makes little sense; his separate latching points are frayed. Here is a passage:

> ...these are teeth
> to punc-
> ture any boy

caught with british lip
to suffer the little come
to (t)hi(s age')s tongue.

Kit Robinson's "Open Letter to Little Flower" is
better. A computer might have written the piece; or did
it drop from a brain with shorn synapses? Also in the
mode of disaffected youth is Stephen Paul Miller. He
writes Magritte-effects, and holds a mirror up to a
rock. There's not much to celebrate in the "ever-crying
marginalia" of life.

Amy Gerstler writes the best poem in the issue--
"Lullaby." There's no monkey-fancy-business, no self-
conscious effort to disjoint syntax or quest after a
pimply surrealism. Her meditation, as she looks down at
her sleeping kid, is as much about herself as lover,
wife, mother, as it is about the babe:

there's only one earth,
where water boils, babies are born and the red sun
falls into a drying meadow inhabited by crowned
cranes. Or seems to. Forgive my dolor, my sweet.
We live wonderful days.

Marjorie Welish writes in a pallid Ashberyan mode: "pale
petals float away." A "moment...overwhelms the
universe." Peter Schjeldahl's "Love Poem" records his
inability to tell his wife he loves her. This poem
could regenerate hordes of tired marriages. There's
also an interview with Schjeldahl. Ed Smith's boredom
leads him to brief, trashy fantasies, very underkeyed.
These things command his attention--being shot and
having a cock up his rear. He's cool: "Imagine pissing
with a hard-on." A vintage Ron Koertge poem follows.
Dumbo teaches 'rithmetic. He's a handicapped soul, with
ghost limbs and a nose job. The faculty like having him
around "because with that physique and color / he meets
government guidelines for all sorts / of minorities and
handicapped." There's a photo-collage by Tom Clark, of
Laurie Anderson's "O Superman."

In Ken Deifik's seven-page "Key Fools," an
adolescent mind is obsessed with good looks, glamour, a
doppelganger, easy mysticisms ("a mystical place, full
of bicycles" is either Heaven or Hell.) This adolescent
snivel is laced with humor. In the 50's and 60's we had
the Warholian dumb stammer, as if we were learning to
mouth our baby syllables again, starting over with Joe
D'Allesandro's primitive word-urge. At least in the
80's, a la Deifik and others, we have once again
embraced language--though possibly for the sake of
destroying it.

A good piece by Tim Dlugos, a masturbatory, hormonal-arousing take on a boy-star in a swimming pool, is reminiscent of David Hockney's work. This is followed by Bernard Welt's cosy "To Tim Dlugos." He thinks he's writing like Frank O'Hara; but he's not. Things are not "fine here on Mt.Idy." Jeff Wright and Greg Masters think they've wasted time getting educations. Masters says it best. Lewis Warsh assumes the persona of a Korean woman abandoned by her lover. David Trinidad writes an understated elegy for a friend. Bob Flanagan's personality takes off into the blue, in the title poem for his latest book:

> Delicious day, I will
> eat you up like
> a mountain of white
> cake, chunk by
>
> chunk. I've got new
> shoe laces. My feet
> slip into my shoes
> over and over again.
>
> So easy. Everything
> pleasing me,
> sliding down my
> throat....

And Terence Winch is ironic about his life:

> I have tons of money & a gorgeous
> air conditioner. Great art hangs
> on my wall. I live a spine tingling life
> of delirious sex & intense happiness.

In a second poem, he undercuts the irony of the first one. He addresses a sleeping trick:

> I think of you with a knot in my stomach.
> I refuse to feel melodramatic.
> I want you to wake up.
> I am hypnotized by departures.

Jack Skelley, pop musician and editor of Barney, demonstrates his mastery of the comic-book mode. His girl responds to his attentions: "I let you go, flopping in my affection, / and plop before you; and you suddenly smile." They drive to the Planetarium where he idealizes her. Steve Benson writes an interior monologue about a youth who keeps coming into the store; some things coalesce, others don't. Michael Friedman's seven "Sonnets" dismay me. They are crammed with clichés. Judging from his picture, he's about seventeen, cute, and probably has only begun to sort the hackneyed out of his life. In these gurgles of style, there's something good.

Towards the back, there's a feature on <u>Kenward Elmslie</u>, complete with poems, mildly funny drawings, and an interview with the ZZZZ-Man. The poems sound like Elmslie retreads. Clever, jazzy, old Aunt Mary-ish ("botheration!") Facile jottings of the mind's flotsam-jetsam: "To night we'll pool our resources, shorn of identity accretions." These poems <u>shamble</u>, to use a word Elmslie likes. Best is a prose poem about kumming on daddy's lap; at least, I think that's what happens. If Elmslie pared things, settled for less than the first little nipple-flip, and pursued that "ultra-violent snit," I wouldn't be so negative.

Wind off with a series of photographs, "Fake Love," of two adolescents having explicit sex. Call one boy New York and the other Los Angeles. Poetry is orgasmic, a leek-ish flow, whether it transpires on Hollywood Boulevard or Union Square. LITTLE CAESAR will come up behind and grab you when you're not looking. It's young and randy. You may not like everything--but you'll find nil Stodge, nil Momentosity, nil Academic Sleaze.

THE NEW YORKER

(March-May 1982). Editor: Howard Moss. 25 West 43rd St., New York, NY 10036. $28 per year.

I've suspected for some time that NEW YORKER poems are quite like NEW YORKER covers, rich in seasons and commuter-hood. This is the journal of the bouffant, canapé life, of a humor that won't crack your makeup or split your sides, and of an easy melancholy over the lost years of your youth in Scarsdale, Montauk, Brooklyn Heights, or Milwaukee. Spring dominates these NEW YORKER covers, as the season is appropriate, nicely setting a glow: suburbanite on tractor-mower trimming his lawn, an old Robert Frostian man asleep beneath a blooming apple tree, a passel of bunnies flashing scuts among the hyacinths and tulips. I'd never realized how shaped and connected, nay, stifled, NEW YORKER poems are by such limitations. I've decided to examine a dozen poems published between March 22, 1982 and May 24, 1982. I have distressing news for the hordes of poets hoping to sell work here.

T. R. Hummer's "Love Poem: The Dispossessed' (22 March) is on early spring. A small river, gray-heated, in "your small gray city," thaws. The chilled poet walks on "a gray stone wall." Down below are the remains of snowbanks. The trees are indefinably gray: "they are all / One tree to me." The poet is "a small man" by a "small river," a figure on an old postcard "mailed years ago" but lost in the post office.

Joseph Brodsky's "Ecologue IV: Winter" (29 March) returns the cover-scene to a dull, cold, muddy day: "In winter, to put it bleakly, Brodsky writes, "Tuesday is Saturday." We dream about nasturtiums and embers smoldering "In dawn's gray ashes." We are sick of winter: "In February, the later it is the lower / the mercury. More time means more cold." We hope to get cold out of our system before spring arrives. Here it is, March 29th, and the rivers are still ice-locked. So are Brodsky's teeth. At least in winter the angels are happy--for then they "are invisible." White on white. If we had the eye-angle, "on high, where they are linking / in white camouflage like Finnish marksmen," we might see them. In John Engel's "Cardinals" (March 29), a fearless red bird enters "the circle" of the poet's thumb and finger. The cardinal escapes, to become a tiny flame across the yard, in "the dark heart of a cedar." Shortly, five other cardinals appear. "The lawns are full of green light." What a great cover! Five red splotches--no, six--and wintry trees bathed in

a spring light.
    The Easter Poem is written by Charles Wright (April
5). It's long, written in the flocked / flickered lines
Wright likes these days:

> Easter again, and a small rain falls
> On the mockingbird and the housefly,
> On the Chevrolet
> In its purple joy
> And the TV antennas huddled across the hillside.

This aches for a cover artist. And I love this
rendition of the pathetic fallacy: Easter's "little
mouths" are all "open into the rain." Wright-riffs
follow: recollections of boyhood days hunting with
"Princess and Buddy working the millet stands / And the
vine-lipped face of the pinewoods." "Linkages" tie
Easters present to Easters past. Also, here is Wright's
ubiquitous sense of a nameless, vaporous doom--he wants
to sit by a riverbank, beneath an evergreen tree, and
gaze "in the face of whatever, / the whatever that's
waiting for me." Spring seems to soften his melancholy,
as gulls whimper over the boathouse, monarch butterflies
cruise flower beds, and "the soft hairs of spring"
thrust up "through the wind." The sun drops "into its
slot without a click."

    W. S. Merwin (April 12) provides a neutered take on
a poet's storm-world. In his reverie (rendered as a
sort of non-cover), his boyhood home isn't there, nor is
the hill he once climbed "to see the night pasture / in
the afternoon in spring." In good Merwin-fashion, he
lifts his eyes above the horizon, the better to see
nothing except a few clouds. For L. M. Rosenberg (April
19) spring uncurls her "first green messages." In a
dark theater, a man brushes the poet's arm--a groin
throb; a gas station attendant lays "a cool hand" (No,
he's not Luke) on a woman's breast. Sanitized sex. Hard
to make a good cover of this one.

    "Spring" is by the poetry editor, Howard Moss.
Good cover material: stalled traffic, with Chevettes
going "sideways in a field," or up "into a cloudless
sky" to escape for home--every stalled commuter's dream.
We are treated to a little diner, a garage, and a
nursery where trees struggle "to produce more leaves."
We reflect: "How gradual spring is here!" Is it because
we've hitherto not slowed down enough to notice?
Haven't NEW YORKER covers been cluing us in for a whole
month, with the irrepressibility of Mary Poppins with a
hyacinth stuck up her vagina, flower-end first?

    Some relief from spring appears in Susan Mitchell's
"Elegy for a Child's Shadow"(April 19), although it too

is cover-art. There's a kid's bike against a tree, with a mother, bench, and shadow. The poem ends with rain "exciting the leaves to stillness." How's that for paradox? David St. John sprawls over two full pages (26 April) with "The Swan at Sheffield Park." Unabashed, he prosily declares: "It is the dim April / Though perhaps no dimmer than any /London April my friend says." The pair ramble up Kew Gardens, observe the orangery, ordinary people, and other sights. They light finally on clouds (rendered coyly as "God's swans."). Later, the sky produces "a curtaining mist." A real swan now creates a "perfect spreading V" on the water. Trite. The swan sails on, leaving nothing but the rain "pocking the empty table / Of the lake." The rest of the poem recounts some risqué women in Chelsea. One, a Soho stripper, gives St. John a real show, a beneath-the-swan-view of down and muff.

Thom Gunn's is the only poem that has nothing in it suitable for a NEW YORKER cover. What a relief! He recalls the laughter of a pair of sisters. The surviving one (the other sister is dead) divorced now tells Gunn her troubles. The visit over, Gunn again hears her laughter, laughter shared with a son: "unchanged, a sweet, / high stumble of the voice, / rudimentary tune."

W. S. Merwin returns with "Coming Back in the Spring" (May 17). Again, a Cover Motif: "tall buildings blue in the distance...with amber light along them ending / in amber light / and their sides shining above the river of cars." Perfect! Even the color-tones are in. He winds off with another Cover Possitility: paired walkers walk faster through the streets than people walking in groups: beyond Union Square a "white tower" lights up "blue and white / during the first few / hours of darkness."

Donna Joy's "Finches, Moths, Herons" seems out of place, on May 24th. It should come earlier, when Joy had faith that spring "would come" and "rosy finches arrow through." She's very sentimental. Her herons are "angels / of a common and amazing sadness."

My conclusions about THE NEW YORKER come as a surprise. I had no idea how single-minded the editor is. Yet, when I told a poet who has appeared numerous times in the magazine, he seemed unsurprised: "Every poet knows what sort of poem he has to write to sell it here." Perhaps I'm naive; but isn't this poet-prostitution? Obviously, America's best-known poets without a qualm scribble these recipe poems. I urge Howard Moss and his elves to retire one of the seasons each year, and make space for about four months of poems that have nothing whatsoever to do with seasons. Later, he might banish poems containing ideas for inspiring covers. THE NEW YORKER could do much better by verse.

THE OHIO REVIEW

No. 27 (1982). Editor: Wayne Dodd. Ohio University, Athens, OH 45701. $10 per year.

1.

We find an insert-chapbook, "Life in Progress," by Bruce Wetterroth. He celebrates a coot, a garter snake with front legs, cicadas, crickets, transparent crabs, a turtle, owl pellets, a crow's wing, spiders, grouse, buzzing flies, field sparrows, Rosaline "ripe as a melon," a cricket in a coal cellar, lobelia, Mozart, a dead shrew "garnished in honeysuckle," swallows on wires, gentians, pine needles, more gentians, a toad, juncos, stray cats, ratsnakes. These pieces teem with wild-life, a veritable bestiary. They are unpretentious, well-fashioned, sensitive, and worth reading.

2.

Poems by Jack Meyers, Lloyd Davis, Donald Junkins, Jeanne Braham, Peter Makuck, Sherry Nothe, Rick Campbell, Lisel Mueller, Celia Watson Strome, Eileen Silver-Lillywhite, Jennifer Rose, Robert Wrigley, Tricia Bauer, Mary Oliver and Ed Ochester say these things, more or less interchangeably: I keep two white cats. Birds with strings of sunlight in their beaks fly through. In a newt's eye you can see the eye of the turtle. My mother's eyes are two grains of rice. The frog's eye, though, is quite poppy. An outdoor toilet sits in a field of wet weeds. My mother saw the smoke and got my brother's belt. We looked for blacksnakes under granite rocks. Green onions make good salads. My father's back. Grandpa smiles on his porch. Hornets in the rafters. I'll sit on your lap in the kitchen. I squat next to the wheel on the floor of the tractor. Those weren't bats. We know bats. Our skin tells us; so does our wide-mouthed mailbox, the curved beak of romance. The kitchen has a secret door. The swing creaks. We hear laughter and the shuffle of cards. You are always arriving at the ice-house, through the uncut

oleanders. Cocoon nests web the trees. I awake to see
my mother's hair. Severed hoses and our lives. Smears
of chicken. Small hunks of straw. Like a pincurl, like
a pulse, like life.

3.

One has the feeling that if there were no furry
creatures in the world, no farms, no oleanders, no
parents to lave with treacly kisses, no William
Wordsworth, no James Wright, no William Stafford, no Rod
McKuen, there would be no OHIO REVIEW. Much of this
work (exceptions are Robert Wrigley, Ed Ochester, Donald
Junkins) is cut from the same gingham bolt with
occasional organdy swatches tossed in. No poem is badly
written. I can't but feel, though, that James Wright,
somewhere in the skies, is blasting his cornet very
hard, in protest.

POETRY

Vol. CXXXIX: No. 6. Vol. XCL: No. 2 (March, May 1982).
Editor: John Frederick Nims. PO Box 4348, Chicago, IL
60680. $20 per year.

When I reviewed POETRY seven years ago for KAYAK, I
found almost nothing in its hoary pages to excite me.
To continue reading up-coming numbers would be an utter
waste of time. But there's a new editor, so I take a
new look, choosing to scrutinize an issue filled with
poets who've appeared before, and an issue of newcomers.
The latter is more interesting than the former.

1.

Robert Beverley Ray starts off the old-comers with
poems reeking of the traditional stuff found in earlier
POETRY magazines: elegant, chatty, and littered with
queen-talk: perhaps, however, let us say first that. We
hear echoes of T. S. Eliot: "As the women discussed old
stories / Organized around long journeys by train."
Easy life-thoughts prevent the reader from being too
introspective: "I am only looking for a reason to be
happy." Polysyllabic, lit'rary words scatter and make

the stodgy reader with cultural pretensions feel secure
(These folk always know what good poetry is: "the slow
elucidation of the mornings." "Confidences that
required / A vast accumulation of other material"). Use
French titles and allusions to amuse the plebes: "Les
Cahiers du Chemin," passacaglia. Eye the boys on the
Spanish Steps. Ray writes tea rather than coffee poems:

> She offered me tea.
> We sat together at a scaled-down table,
> Two identical white demi-tasse cups.

Numerous lines are useful as ironic commentaries on such
work: POETRY poems reflect "a knowledge that is not
located anyplace in particular / But is merely a
consequence of the system. The details are
interchangeable...." Poems are "a flurry of assurances,
and a feeling of adequacy / Not lightly assumed." The
"smell of the ice on the windowframes /Bears some
relation to something...." It helps to see writing "as
a kind of research, / Or as music that can be extended /
Without implying any direction...." None of these poems
produce "real description, but only / Ideal fragments,
detachable." Texts are "misplaced" by "the mildest
sort of metapysics."

Ray is followed by Thomas P. Lynch with some
grandmother and widow poems, and a poem about a dog with
a pearlescent cataract blooming in his one good eye.
Sarah Provost nastily shoots down "archetypal romance,"
but blows it in the last line, unable as she is to
resist an old chestnut: "For God's sake hold your tongue
/ and let me love!" Jerald Bullis contributes a nature
poem, "Trumansburg Creek," spoiled by self-conscious
music: glenlet, knurling, rootgnarls, glisters, and
"frost your peeping enfolds to, frog," and "dew, deer
you / Wander in the duskflumes...." His "Approaching
Dinner" is better, despite the closing quasi-sermon.
Gary Soto scribbles to his daughter. Sandra Gilbert eats
her words, and meditates on blood pressure. She handles
the frayed You Poem with intensity. Her blood-pressure
kit becomes a loathsome serpent with "acid tongue"
flicking an old man's cheekbones, "whipping his whole
body."

2.

Brooks Haxton is the first poet appearing in the
Newcomers' issue. He provides a terrific long poem,
"Breakfast Ex Animo," about getting up the courage to
run to the henhouse to see what's disturbing, and
possibly killing, the birds. He writes a contemporary
mock-heroic poem, so good you'll want to read it aloud.
The piece is a dozen pages long. Yes, it is

anachronistic--and has a tie-in with older genres (Chaucer wrote beast-fowl mock-epic poems). Haxton transcends the limitations. Naomi Shihab Nye writes about all the catalogues reaching her house, and about a man who clips trees. Carol Henrie's topics are crows on the road during a rain, death, and mom's fear when kids get home late from school. John Vernon has four poems centered in rural life. Changes are his theme. The best poem is "Mud Man" (a man in a tree after a flood observes another man drown in mud) and "Barns Collapsing."

In a weak poem, Andrew Hudgins, speaking through John James Audubon, the naturalist, considers the plight of a bittern. Wing Tek Lum and Julia Lavarez are competent but dull. Lavarez, though, has a knack for assembling details; she may be better at fiction than poetry. Michael Hoffman writes a good workshop poem on "White Noise." I wish he had let his sense for wild motion and verve really dance. Red Hawk likes buffalo and carnage in the West. Some of his touches are marvellous:

> Flank shivers spread for miles like waves
> across an ocean of wet fur.
> The bulls move to the edge of a forming circle.
> Suddenly
> there are the wolves....

His poem about the hen-house has a pair of silly moments: as he leaves, his sweetie kisses him ("your kiss was full of tongue") and holds "4 cold, brown-speckled eggs" against his cheek. That's a lot of eggs for one hand.

Ann Nicodemus Carpenter takes interesting risks. In "Motel" she develops a nervy metaphor. Being inside a Ramada Inn is like being clapped shut inside a book. In "Depreciation," a "wind-up mother," a "life-sized stuffed-up father," and a "wornout lover" end up in a garage sale. Her "Ars Poetica" is terrific: poems as turtle eggs, as bear cubs, and, finally, as calamitous things lounging about the house, "half-stoned, / Taking short trips in manila envelopes, /Calling home for return postage." She hits a nerve. J. P. White has three poems, touched with a quality reminiscent of Ed Dorn's poems. He's pretty loquacious though, and doesn't invite re-reading. His insistence on the iamb gets him into trouble.

On the whole, this "First Appearances" issue is miles ahead of the other one.

Vol.XXIII:4 (Winter 1982-1983). Editor: David Wagoner.
Editorial Consultants: Nelson Bentley, William H.
Matchett, William Matthews. 4045 Brooklyn Ave NE,
University of Washington, Seattle. WA 98105. $8 per year
(4 issues).

22 poets. 50 pages of verse. 41 poems.
Fundamentalist American Verse, Compost Verse, Mulch
Poetry, fashioned around the objects and sentiments dear
to the Frosts and Falwells of poetry--virtues of family
life, much bucolicism (with nary a nod towards the city
except to condemn same), much first person, much
recollection of trivial events and persons, a chaste,
decorous language (night, we read, like a stray dog
"lifts its leg / on the yellow pansies." This is about
as outrè as these poems get. When one poet reports his
"jock-itch," we are, as Chaucer said, "astonied."), an
occasional Swatch of Kulchur (Verdi, Schumann, Van
Gogh's ear, "the golden birds of Yeats"), easy free
verse forms and limpid iambs....all
comfortable...comfortable.

The living mentor of these interchangeable writings
is William Stafford, who appears with two poems: one is
especially family-riddled and chummy: Aunt Helen sews
"all day" on a comforter stitched from pieces of
Grandma's dresses. She sews, she says, for the whole
family--and for Dorothy Stafford, "that we may be warm
in the house by the tracks." Stafford remembers a well
where son Kim "almost fell in," and, with a sigh,
recalls the lump beneath the snow where Bret's tiny car
lay nestled through one winter. The unifying theme is
"long distance"--of telephone and time.

Perhaps a partial listing of the gimcrack in these
poems will serve as a commentary on the limitations:
eggs, willows, fields, hills, seedbeds, feather
mattresses, clocks, beeches and chestnuts, fists of
roots gripping boulders, pie-safes and cupboards,
porches, truckstops, melancholy far-off trains,
whimpering family puppies, old apple trees, plums,
belled cows, feathers in a mattress, the wolf at the
door, raccoons in the garbage, toads, etcetera. Now,
paste in some treacly sentiments, drop warm salty tears
on your apron or your denim workshirt, and declare that
you are one with the ancestors--people of the soil--who
have slipped off as Eternal Compost.

25 poems allude to members of the poets' families,
both dead and alive. Grandfolks come in for a lot of

attention, as do daughters and sons. Some twenty pieces employ the moon for decor. These are among the occupations extolled: hammering studs, barbering "soft archipelagoes of hair," boxing, taking a shower, carving red cedar, staking tomatoes and strawberries, picking peas, being schoolboys, having babies, cormorant-watching, naming wood-flowers, waiting for customers, scouring kitchen pots, laying down linoleum...

Mediocre poets are apt to condemn themselves from their own mouths better than any critic can. I take these lines at random, all from different poems:

"You need something / to happen."

"I am plain as black ink on a white page."

"It is the gut note sweet with suffering."

"That night my sophomore date wanted kisses."

"That heart is academic."

"It looked all right on the map."

"It's where Ada Beare sat every afternoon talking to strangers."

"Neat as a puzzle...cut of feebleminded stars."

"We dragged each other under."

"I wish they would eat me whole."

"My daughter cartwheeling in her own backyard."

"Ruth feeds sparrows."

"The tadpoles gather."

These lines are, I admit, out of context; yet they do not entirely misrepresent the poems in which they appear. My method, inspired by Matthew Arnold's once much-vaunted Touchstone Method, is now much out of favor. Perhaps it is time to restore it as an oven thermometer of verse, or for taking rectal temperatures at gatherings of poet-tadpoles.

One poem, "Helix Aspersa" is almost a parody of the Humus School. Anita Endrezze-Danielson treats us to encyclopedia information on snails. She reassures us that the creature "has no insight:"

Observe its two front tentacles
which scent leaf-mold and lance leaf.
Its two longer tentacles are feeble eyes,
sensing only the light
which fogs its lusterless shell,
and the shadows that are boneless and flourishing.

Daniel Hoffman supplies a couple of Culture Poems--
re: British schoolboys wearing their blazers and an
ancient French chapel at Fontaine-les-Dijon. These seem
out of place.

During rare moments when Mulch-poets try to be
zippy, the results seem anachronistic. The first stanza
of "Backing up on the Freeway," by Edward Kleinschmidt
is complete with flapper-talk and echoes of 1950's TV
commercials:

We do this outrage of the tv,
this gee whiz to the streetwise,
tsk tsk to the poptops, and hold
no high noses, no, no high noses.

The few good poems are these: "The Wife," by
William Chamberlain, has some fresh, ironic moments: "My
wife is the best joke,/ and if she is here I/ am lord of
rain in a drab town." Carolyn Reynolds Miller's "Ma
Bete" is a wonderfully vicious and poignant account of
the beauty and the beast:

Every night he sleeps in different directions
so she, stumbling lonely, will not catch him by
    surprise.
He might take her for a snowrabbit and tear her
    belly.
Tonight the very room he chooses without reason
she hides in, weeping. He must stop and listen.
It is like the moon's rain falling into his heart.
When he takes hold of the door, he is shocked by grie
in the silver knob. Through his hide
he sees her lying frail as a broken bird
and naked. She will not know when he enters,
her face a velvet mask
on which she has painted
the face of a beast.

Joyce Quick's "Poet's Holdup" should be read at all
poetry readings. Richard Ronan writes with energy of two
lovers (male, I gather) getting it on in a forest. The
lyric evokes sex-smells via natural images and odors.
How did this one ever sneak past the conservative
editor? Perhaps because Ronan skillfully and shrewdly
masked the real event of the poem, inviting an R rather
than an X rating?

Among the featured(but not necessarily the best) poets are these: Rodney Jones, William Stafford, Susan Stewart, Daniel Hoffman, Brian Swann, and Christine Gebhard.

What amazes one about a magazine so seemingly singleminded as POETRY NORTHWEST is its longevity and its exalted reputation. Do its subscribers actually read the verse published here? Until there is a massive turning from the "I Poem" and the related trivia, such journals as this (and they are currently numerous) will flourish. I'm ready to go back to A. E. Housman, Dante Gabriel Rossetti, Henry Wadsworth Longfellow, and Algernon Charles Swinburne! Are you coming with me? I'm sick of clearing out that pasture spring.

Vol. VI: No. 4 (July 1982).   Editor: E. V. Griffith.
3118 K St., Eureka, CA 95501. $7.50 for 4 issues.

After six years of vigorous effort, E. V. Griffith has established POETRY NOW as a generous showcase for poets both known and unknown.   No poetry journal features so many poets per issue--131 writers are in this number, an amazing representation by any standard. In an interview, Griffith features David Ray.   He "reviews" recent books by these poets: Cary Waterman, Dave Etter, Vern Rutsala, Kathleen Spivack, Franz Douskey, John Ashbery, and William Dickey.   There's a spread of translations, plus half a dozen featured "newcomers."   Griffith publishes nearly 500 poets per year.

Given so rich a feast, one might expect to see many currents represented.   What we have are home-cooked poems-- beef and taters,   thick starchy soups,   much potato salad, and meringue pies heaped with creams and glazes. There's little experimental or new.   These poems read the way American poems have for decades--very Frostian, very denotative, very much of mundane lives, and of the memories of parents and siblings.   Styles, modes,   themes,   and   subjects   are   too   often indistinguishable one from the other. A basic Poetry Chevrolet with interchangeable parts.

Christopher Bursk writes predictably of a father and son rock-hopping, with a Jesus-motif:

Matt closes his eyes
and lets his legs deliver him.
I run on top of the water,
on tips of rocks just under the waves.

Stephen Stepanchev does a nicely satiric take on our wish to "procreate in beauty," as a sexy youth leans against a tree.   In actual fact, his beauty is marred by a missing front tooth.   The tree is an apricot clustered with fruit (scroti?).   So much for sex. Mark Halperin unwittingly gives the finger to most of these poems. They "take small bites."   Ann Darr bites well, recalling an early boyfriend who was killed on his motorcycle. After all these years, his voice still tingles her nipples.   And there's a vintage Charles Bukowski piece: "a man in his late fifties has to / pace himself.   Some women think a pecker is an / everlasting thing." William Matthews mixes tones over the telephone, with a frosty nastiness.   James Schevill writes as Gutzon

Borglum carves those heads on Mt. Rushmore. Ted Kooser
supplies a laid-back, short take on Voyager II. W. R.
Moses deliquesces in the Frostian mode on "Scrawny
blueberries" and "one of those sad-sweet, heart-tugging
specimens / Of the derelict: a time-shattered rowboat."

Five pages of commonplace prose poems, most of them
celebrating the trivial, ensue. All short-circuit.
Nance Van Winckel's boy stands under a steel bridge,
feeds ducks, and

> thinks about a girl
> he loves
> or could love
> all night under
> a different sort of bridge.

Janet Flanders writes about a teacher, Miss Blessing,
and a mean kid she mistreats. John Oliver Simon shouts
"up into the clear reflected forest" along the Jedediah
River; some of his positives and his negatives are
visible. Cynthia Brown Dwyer's "The Blue-Eyed Persian
Plumber" is fresh, with realistic details. So is an
ejaculation by Marge Piercy. Ronald Koertge has fun
dressing up in his mother's underwear. Michael Hogan
celebrates cottonwoods, the banality of life, and poems
"from everywhere inside you." Lyn Coffin escapes from
the locker room and the pressures of boy-cock and a
coach's boy-obsessions. The juvenile hero has first sex
with a girl, "catches on like fire," and is saved from a
homosexual life. Very up-beat. Stuart Dybek walks
home through a papaya grove, his "dizzy eardrum busted /
diving for conch." He stuffs his shirt full of sticky
fruit. Reg Saner pulls off sparrow heads, "common as
popping your knuckles." Lyn Lifshin continues the tacky
myth of herself as a perpetual-motion sex machine.
There's a moving elegy by Norma Farber on the Israeli
athletes killed in Munich in 1972.

Too often in these pages sentiment and bad writing
mix: George montgomery wants "to be in" Linda,

> like a young
> Glen Miller
> would want
> to be
> in a band.

These line breaks are wretched. Linda Pastan
writes about losing a dog:

> when my
> dog died and

        I cried too much
        too long

<u>Wanda</u> <u>Coleman</u> spins off a short sex poem in quasi-black
lingo. She winds up with these hard <u>C</u> sounds, à la the
typing exercise manual:

        cuz their bodies
        couldn't generate
        enuff heat to copulate
        comfortably.

    POETRY NOW prefers the conservative poem. Despite
an occasional kinkiness (Bukowski and Koertge), the
drift is towards apple-pie values and the American way.
The fact that <u>Richard</u> <u>Eberhart</u> starts off this issue (he
verges on doggerel) symbolizes the poems to follow.
And yet, once I say all this, there's much in POETRY NOW
you will enjoy. For the Newcomers alone it is worth a
subscription. If you send poems, though, don't be too
far out and bizarre.

THE PUSHCART PRIZES

THE PUSHCART PRIZE VII: BEST OF THE SMALL PRESSES: An Annual Small Press Reader. Editor: Bill Henderson. Poetry Editors: Gerald Stern and Carolyn Forché. Pushcart Press (paper ed. Avon Books), PO Box 380, Wainscott, NY 11975. 568pp. $22

I've never understood that old cliché "tongue in cheek." If you thrust the tip of your tongue against your right cheek, does that carry less of an onus than if you thrust it against the left? In either case, I suppose, you convey an unspoken suspicion of being had, or taken in--or that you are about to have someone, or take them in. That's how I feel after plowing through this 7th Pushcart compendium. What I've suspected to be true for other years is more than ever true this year: PUSHCART unabashedly reflects conservative tastes. True, there are minimal nods to minority writers, gays, and obscure presses. Tokenism. Their favored magazines (APR, POETRY, ANTAEUS, IOWA REVIEW, YALE REVIEW) have held chloroformed hankies over our faces, and will probably go on doing so until screams of outrage pierce the smog shrouding Mt. Olympus. I have criticized PUSHCART prose elsewhere, and will concentrate on the poetry, which is, alas, much inferior to the prose.

I agree with the editors that Charles Wright deserves a hundred bucks as the "lead" poet--if you favor poems that perpetuate a tradition running from Dante to Ezra Pound. If you are looking elsewhere, though, you might give the prize to Simon Ortiz (more about him later). A long chunk of Wright's last book THE SOUTHERN CROSS, appearing first in THE PARIS REVIEW, is featured. Wright has skill, passion, and intelligence. He seems to have matured, to have abandoned some of the self-pity marring earlier books. There's humor, and an energy that salts the moments before they drift off into a fashionable angst. The sequence is loose--the magic emerges within the separate brief sections where Wright allows himself pitches of emotion and invention.

The remaining poets (about 30 of them) are a mix of names known and unknown. The knowns are inferior to the unknowns. The former are here, I'd say, as window-dressing. Featured are poets who slop frequently at troughs provided by ANTAEUS, APR, HUDSON REVIEW, and SOUTHERN REVIEW. The only overt collusion I detect is that Sharon Olds nominates Philip Levine who nominates Sharon Olds. Otherwise, buddy-strokes are kept semi-visible. There's plenty of rot at the core of American poetry--if these prize selections are representative.

67

Derek Walcott loves pretentious jawbreaking phrases more than he does watching that bull hump Europa. To appreciate his randy voyeurism you must wade through such suet as this: "luminously rumpled," "insatiably promiscuous," "proper distance," "anagrammed in stars." One hears echoes of the brassier music of old Yeats. Yet, the final lines pinning the bull to the stars is quite stunning. William Pitt Root, in an effective imitation of Robinson Jeffers, recalls Jefferson truisms: the old poet built a house of boulders at Big Sur, and that he wrote a famous poem about a hawk.

Gary Soto supplies a predictable poem about illegal aliens jogging over the border. Prize-winning poet and Cal Berkeley Professor Soto gets mistaken for one of the wet-backs and has to flee the patrol. Soto reaches for cosmic stuff. C. K. Williams follows with a lengthy long-liner spinning out the passivity and gloom we expect from him. A paraplegic Vietnam vet tips over in his wheel-chair. Poet glimpses the man's "poor, blunt pud, tiny, terrified, retracted...almost invisible in the sparse genital hair." His pants, unfortunately, get ripped off by a friend trying to right him. If Sinclair Lewis were still alive, and if he wrote poetry, this is the kind he'd write.

Elizabeth Thomas employs those awful "I" phrases as if they are still in fashion. When a little energy creeps in, she deadens it with some arty phrase, viz., dead hens hang "like bright / corsages" from killer-dog jaws. Thomas is a weak tinter, to borrow an image from tie-dying. Even sexual moments are aqua-tinted. Here she seems to be writing about cunnilingus: "I wrap your hair / like wet grass around my thighs. / It is one woman after another." Sharon Olds, one of the minor queen-bees of this volume, spoils a stark event (a small daughter is missing) by repeating 25 first-person tags in nearly as many lines. These become motley, reminiscent of those scraps of cloth fools use to ornament their costumes. She also likes touches of Momentosity. Here's one borrowed from the old radio villain The Shadow, and/or E. A. Poe, George Eliot, or Thomas Hardy: her quest, she informs us, is "to know where it is, the evil in the / human heart."

Stanley Kunitz displays one of his lesser efforts, ripped off, perhaps, from D. H. Lawrence. His metaphor of entwined snakes as "a brazen love-knot" is frayed-- so are the cosmological touches. Michael Harper is embarassingly trivial. He writes chummily of giving a reading in NYC during a blizzard, of being introduced by Galway Kinnell, and of riding a horse around Central Park. He does a bit of tame in-house thinking about James Wright and Philip Levine. Harper's poem opens so

badly, afflicted as it is with prepositionitis, it could
serve as a model for lousy writing in workshops. I've
underlined the prepositions:

> In the year of the blizzard
> In the month of February
> I have traipsed up the middle
> of Lexington Avenue, a spectacular
> middle passage in the snow
> to my own poetry reading....

Stephen Berg isn't really fair to himself,
inserting, as he does, a most risky line, of the self-
revealing and condemnatory sort critics love to sniff
out. Berg writes: "Nobody would call it poetry." His
poem, I fear, fulfills his judgment well. Berg's ear is
one of the worst. He has a real affection for dead line-
endings: sky, abruptly, gloomy, embroidery, high, when
I.... And this phrase is a nadir: "reminds me of when
I...." I'd hoped Mary Oliver would be better; but her
Eve-confronting-that-snake-poem, alas, has little in it
to invite a second look. Jorie Graham leads me to ask
why there are such dreadful lapses of taste and double
entendres in these poems. Is it that the journals
troughing these writers (most of them in their 30's or
40's) swill them so early they feel they no longer are
apprentice poets? Has "success" come too soon?

Back to Graham, who pulls off a neat one: She is
given some "bottom fish" by a neighbor. (I resist the
sexual inuendoes). She spins these over-wrought, pompous
life-notes: The frozen fish (she has "a choir of them,"
she informs us, singing their muddy bottom notes) become
"speechless, angelic /instruments." "By our life-lumps,"
as old Whitman might have exclaimed, "What do they play?
Music of the spheres?" No. Music of the mud! We humans
are mud, and no matter how much we wish to "fall out of
this world" we merely sink deeper into "muddy daylight."

David Ignatow leans back in his chair, stretches
his legs over his bed, and thinks of his long-dead
father listening to opera. Rossini stimulates some
ghost-wrestling. Ignatow admonishes his dead dad to stop
bugging him--they are both lonely old men. Linda Pastan
is another poet who loves dipping little crullers
fashioned out of those "I" phrases run rampant into her
morning coffee. Pastan laces the brew with fashionable
fat dollops of self-pity.

Fresh air enters with Leo Romero. His Escolastica
loses her leg, gets a wooden one, and marries her man
anyway, astounding the gossips by her success as wife
and mother. This poem hurts. It reads like a Mexican
Spoon River Anthology piece. I loved Katha Pollitt's

"Turning Thirty." A still girlishly-vibrant woman, a loner, realizes she is aging; but as she rides a train to her next lover her elan is infectuous. Paul Zimmer continues the myth of "Paul Zimmer" with yet another Zimmer Poem. There's little to praise or to damn. Our drifting Zimmer "knows nothing and feels little. / He has never been anywhere / And fears where he is going." Perhaps reading FROM HERE TO ETERNITY will take him somewhere. I hope so. To a Salvation Army Store?

Kate Daniels tries hard to deal with the fact that her dead father (how many poems about dead dads can American poetry stand in a year?) was a louse. She wants to lie down in the wrinkles of an ugly taxi-driver's face and find out what she really thinks about pop. They do look a lot alike--dad and cabbie. She finally ends up in her dad's lap, in a vision, and decides she liked him--and she says this movingly.

You'll enjoy Hayden Carruth's nostalgia piece about jazz greats available only on scratched records. Those riffs imparted an "indispensable rightness in the wrong / of eternity." James Wright's posthumous "The Journey" is easily the best poem. Wright could fashion one of those Fulbright Poems (here he is in Anghiari, Italy) into something marvellous and strange--often by focusing on some detail. He meditates on a spider in a dusty web. Naomi Shihab Nye writes unpretentiously about a child's fear of dying. I am moved, despite the presence of ghastly workshop phrases: sickening pattern...strange confidence...unanswerable woes.

How a poem as bad as Marcia Southwick's gets published boggles the mind. Connections? Luck? An attractive picture sent along with submissions? I confess, I don't know. "The Body" is a tedious poem frosted with pretentious language and a trite central idea. Autumn comes always, and is like our life, as we age and tire of our bodies. Southwick loves dull pathetic fallacies: grass is "shy", autumn leaves "contain within them the instructions / for falling." (What would a biologist say about the tautology of this last one?). She'd like to sail off into the sky "which must be pure / as a future without sins...." Anyone for paper airplanes folded out of Pushcart poems?

With relief I turn to Linda Gregg's "Being with Men." Gregg doesn't fuck around, and requires only a few simple lines to shaft home. You'll keep thinking about this one. Larry Levis, who may have inspired some of the weakest of these Pushcart poems, resucitates Walt Whitman as a drug-high daughter, a taciturn Malibu beach-boy, and an old homosexual running a Tilt-a-Whirl. When Levis transforms Whitman into a Charlie Parker fan,

I run to the woods, strip, sit under a tree, and admire
my navel. I know Walt better than that.

One of the daddies of the first-person experiential
poem, Philip Levine, rings in with "The Body Electric"
(thanks again, Walt Whitman). Here is Levine's
characteristically tacky setting (cheap waitress, cheap
cafè, red-necks); the sentimentality (the poet sits
there, he says, like a big weepy peeled onion); and the
surcease from stagnation in potential violence (as he
gets up to walk out to "North Indemnity Avenue," he
hopes a car will hit him when he gets there). It's too
easy. His body electric holds a pretty dim bulb, Walt.

At last, Simon Ortiz has a real subject--the
decimation of American Indians. His style is lean,
machete-sharp. And he eschews the phony Wordsworthian
takes on nature loved by American poets as primitives.
His are not ugh natives enamored of the moon, etc. His
people are victims of the Vietnam war, poverty,
exploitation, and disease. None of this is
sentimentalized; nor does Ortiz forgo craftsmanship for
propaganda. The frame event is the slaughtering of over
125 peaceful natives, at Sand Creek, Colorado, in 1864,
a stark image for his rage.

There is little in Puschart VII to celebrate.
There has to be better work around. The editors might
better search the host of little mags not represented:
LITTLE CAESAR, THE WORMWOOD REVIEW, GARGOYLE, CONTACT
II, SOUP, PULPSMITH, THE REAPER, RACCOON. And they might
broaden the spectrum of judges and recommenders. They
might also eschew what seems like tokenism--a sprinkling
of Chicanos, blacks, gays, feminists, obscure presses.
The result now is a veneer of liberalism, glossy,
shallow. The journals showcased are conservative, with
Eastern or Southern bases. Why? Because so few writers
subscribe to magazines? The ones they read they
probably read in libraries, or they see contributors'
copies. Librarians are notorious for subscribing to the
same dull journals over and over. Ditto for Poetry
Center libraries and reading rooms. Things will get
better? Don't count on it. The Pushcart editors may say
they feature the best work written today. I disagree!
This volume is a travesty. To assist (ie., read
brainwash) reviewers, the publisher packs his fat volume
with laudatory tear-sheets of positive notices from
these biggies: PUBLISHER'S WEEKLY, BOOKLIST, AND KIRKUS.
TIME may not be far behind. Placebo. Placebo. Placebo.

P.S. I've just examined PUSHCART's competitor, THE
RANDOM REVIEW 1982, and find the same dismal drift. The
same middle-aged writers are here (Charles Wright, C.

K. Williams, Katha Pollitt) and most of the magazines
(ANTAEUS, PARIS REVIEW, FIELD, NEW YORKER, YALE REVIEW,
etc.). Another travesty.

QUARTERLY REVIEW OF LITERATURE

Vols. XII & XIII (1981 & 1982). Editors: T. and R.
Weiss. 26 Haslet Ave., Princeton, NJ, 08540. $10 per
copy, or $15 for 2 issues.

After thirty odd years of publishing, QRL changed
from a traditional literary magazine to one that
features five poets per issue, once per year, with
approximately seventy-five poems per poet. Each is paid
$500. (Note: Poets submitting work must subscribe to
the series). Two poets in each issue are foreign. These
translations (of Lars Gustafsson, Wistawa Szymborksa, So
Chongju, and Carlos Nejar) are neither better nor worse
than most translations of foreign poets.

Half of the poets appear with first books; the
others boast earlier publications. Again, QRL deserves
praise for eschewing the tried and the true. Only one
writer, so far as I can tell, hails from Princeton,
where editor Weiss hangs his hat. And there is a
geographical balance: Thompson, with a Ph. D. from the
University of Wisconsin, teaches in Hawaii; David Barton
has a Ph.D. from Stanford and teaches in Atlanta;
Macinnes hails from England (educated at Oxford), but
has lived here twenty-five years; Hirshfield teaches in
California; Bursk hails from Cambridge, Massachusetts;
Bouvard, with an MA in Creative Writing and a Ph.D. in
Government, is chair of the Political Science department
at Regis College. Obviously, unless you have a good
degree of some sort your chances of selling a manuscript
to QRL would seem limited. Well, just how good are
these professor-teacher writers?

JANE HIRSHFIELD ("Alaya")

Hirshfield achieves scattered moments of originality in an otherwise pretty placid slough of feelings and concerns. She likes appearing as a Ceres of poetry--her title "Alaya," a Sanskrit term meaning "the consciousness which is the store house of experience," is, she says, "a place where seed-grain is kept, held for the next season's crops--as the way experience travels forward in time." This leaden seriousness, alas, ruins her poems. She loves ruminating in meadows, until Big Thoughts spew forth. And her numerous "yous" are vaporous. She also favors cultural references from college courses: Hermes, Proteus, Vermeer, Urdu poetry, Troy, Stonehenge, and the Parthenon. She also loves obvious Oriental poets and their verse forms. Most of her work is maimed by self-conscious literary phrases, either confused or commonplace: "one voice, many mouths, / we are many even alone"; "it. . .rained through my tongue" (the tongue as sieve?); life is a thread; and the "sum and force of years" confronts us all. On the positive side, her "Suite For Four Hands," despite the sentimental "yous" inserted like raisins in cow-flops, moves to a strong image: a toy boat fashioned from a walnut shell. "Remnants," an elegy for James Wright, has an impressive final stanza. Hirshfield, I hope, will become more self-critical as she keeps writing.

CHRISTOPHER BURSK ("Little Harbor")

Bursk is a talented, unassuming poet who avoids the fancy pyrotechnics Hirshfield loves. He writes relaxed, sensitive recollections of his childhood. Easy to grasp, these resemble those SATURDAY EVENING POST covers Norman Rockwell used to draw. Bursk likes tie-ins between himself and his progenitors. Life is a matter of carpentry, of joining, of pounding those nails in straight. He builds a tree house with his sons: "unto the 3d and 4th generations of those who pound nails straight and do their own carpentry...." Bursk is gifted at opening lines: "The teachers do something else with their hands in the summer"; "at last I am old enough to bike across Jerusalem Road"; "to get to sleep / my son and I must first say goodnight to his letter blocks." Will the real Norman Rockwell stand up?

MARGUERITE GUZMAN BOUVARD ("Journeys Over Water")

A

I enter myself. I see contours. I have suffered. I have been the enemy. I thank the morning glory. I bounce and sway. I have been a panther. I wondered how. I sat in the livingroom. I scaled the garage roof. I watch my cousin hike for miles.

B

You ran. You wept. You cross your legs. You speak. You dream. You lift the barrel of your lens. You rode alone. You were an empty shoe. You travelled lightly. You tell me how.

PHYLLIS THOMPSON ("What the Land Gave")

Thompson writes with a never-flagging energy. She is a pro with three books to her credit and much publication in magazines, and with many travels and fellowships. Her ear for cadences is usually right--meat-cleaverish rhythms drenched in stiff draughts of literary geritol, cadences of the stentorian sort one imagines that ancient Queen Bodicaea must have used on her troops before she was tied to four horses and driven madly off in all directions. Thompson is no dainty feminine poem-swinger. Well, let's look at some of her Purcellean, Rilkean, Yeatsian strummings and carryings-on.

First one soon discovers that this poet takes herself most seriously. She has "always been a church-goer," she confesses. For her, "work" is "prayer...writing a poem is an act of praise." She is "a religious poet." Well, there are many ways of dividing loaves and fishes. A mark of her work is what I shall call Cope and Mitre Trappings--all those goodies in poems straining for the ecclesiastical, the pompous, the universal. Her grand moments are seldom earned. They are failed efforts meant to jack us up.

Consider a poem to John Logan (Thompson likes writing poems to friends--a minor malady in itself)--"The River." To accommodate her inflated feelings for the older poet, she has to inflate nature. The dear old Susquehanna River has an "onwandering way"--so "onwandering" that "it can be thought of as common speech." That's pretty forced--the result is carp

rather than swordfish. Her river is "fair" (as Edmund
Spenser said of the Thames before it was polluted). A
"flow of low bells" are "ringing singly downstream"
(more decorations for ye olde bishoppe's cope).
Thompson hears "the plainsong of all water." Towards
the end, sentimental, she pulls out the organ-stops,
wafts her abstractions and smoking censors, and loads in
an allusion to one of W. B. Yeats's more obvious lines:

> Of all men I know, John, yours is that voice
> I can call to mind anywhere from my deep heart,
> The serious and the ordinary
> Plainsong that grows out of but beyond weeping and
>   triumph,
> Diminishes guilt, and can reduce even heroic love
>   or failure
> To the same unasking simplicity of clear music
> As of river water lapping weeds on a low shore....

She avoids concrete imagery, preferring vague
leaves, berries, and "everlasting" mountains. She thus
sanitizes and makes her world prayer-book palatable.
God--and He appears a lot--is also neutered and vague.
So with her many sexual moments: while she seems to have
copulated much, she treacles erotical moments o'er with
too much sweetness, eschewing sweat, mucus, and other
glandular excretions fair or foul. When she gives one
lover "bruised guavas" (testicles?) we aren't much
moved. Her best erotic moments are winsomely naive. Here
she is either been busy at cunnilingus or fellatio:
pearls "tenderly rubbed under my lips...this soft wax
feeling...the smell of humid summer fallen...." This
might have been written by Mary Poppins using her
umbrella handle whilst casting her eyes upon the clouds.
One particular image, ubiquitous, of hands, stifles
through its repetitions.

I want to like Thompson's work more. On a first
reading she is impressive, and provides enough energy to
make you feel she's not entirely adrift in Waffle-Land.
It's the lumber she's acquired from much dwelling in
Academic Palaces (those of Spenser, Rilke, Tennyson,
Yeats) that does her in.

DAVID BARTON   ("Surviving the Cold")

The editors would have served Barton better had
they persuaded him to forgo the first 20 of these poems
which read like juvenalia. The final 10 though, are
pretty good. He chatters of self and trivial events
almost as if he were writing items for some small-town
newspaper: wolves are "driven south" by hunger and

disease;" he tires of "being alone"; he finds "tiny
dead ants in the salt"; bird-sightings hereabouts "are
fewer each year"; John, a raiser of "inbred hens," is
now a student at Harvard. Barton is overly-fond of
fancy verbs and adverbs. Also too evident is a device he
picked up in lit classes, a means of ending poems in a
hortatory Shakespearean-Yeatsian manner, with a flurry
of polysyllabic words. Here are the last two lines of
"Plum Island." He's writing about "unnamed, flourishing,
/ vastly immaculate things." This is like trying to get
four tennis balls in your mouth at once. "Bird Skulls"
concludes with "lyrical things / incessantly shaping //
the air." More? He observes(in "The Western Door")
"sparse acres of wild oat / and wild unsettling tares."
He also echoes one of the hoariest and most sterile of
verse takes--the delay of the first person verb phrase
until the second or third line, tarnished echoes of
"arms and the man, I sing": "Above Point Conception, I
walk"; "Waking toward morning...I look"; "Sow-necked
and sallow, I mope." Barton is at his best when he
confronts latent violence in nature. This is good:

> Winter whittles at the day
> until nothing is left
> but bones in an owl's gut....

And here he describes frogs in a marsh: "some curl
together / in their spawn; some droop like genitals, /
congenitally fat / and swelling." In "Late Autumn" he
recalls his father crushing a marsh crane. At moments
this poem is beautiful:

> I finally found myself sitting
> on an embankment, watching
> slugs by a stone, shale flakes
> clacking below the talus.
> The manzanita rattled like
> breakwater.

Barton has a lot of maturing to do. If he can dump most
of the mannerisms and trust his own attitudes, he will
be a terrific poet. Right now, despite signs of vigor
and a special imagination, he writes postures, mainly
literary and conceptual.

MAIRI MACINNES ("Herring, Oatmeal, Milk and Salt")

By far the best of these poets is the English
writer Mairi Macinnes. She's an unabashed
traditionalist who writes with ease, clarity, and skill.

There's no straining after the solipsistic "I" (although her poems are experiential). She recalls the Georgian poets Walter De la Mare, Harold Munro, and Ralph Hodgson. She is a bucolic poet. In "Articles of Belief" she supplies a credo of sorts. "Many writers," she observes, see "clarity" as peeling an orange, "triumphantly" revealing the segments beneath. She used to be more sanguine about such clarity when she was a schoolgirl in a "green world, and heard amazing words / That put things in their place." Today, though, less sanguine, she still seeks clarity when she "manufactures" the objects she writes of. Occasionally, she recalls one of my favorite poets, <u>Stevie Smith</u>, but without Smith's memorable bite and ironic thrust. "Running in the Park," for example, evokes Stevie Smith's child-world. She's tough. Here she writes of pressures from a mother she continues to fail:

> Like a great coarse clod I finger her desires,
> And snivel to recall how they finally burst out
> And walked up and down the earth, looking for a
> home.

She attends an ill son's bedside:

> ...the swollen feverish lids
> And hands unloosened by the loosened mouth,
> Until, all expectation foiled,
> I saw unfold
> A new landscape in him,
> Cluttered with its own unuttered sound.

Macinnes' verse music is intimate, often complex, and always sure. Here is a fine passage crisp with an Anglo-Saxon sound:

> But me--I'm stones and salt,
> I'm running bones.
> My body's a pod of dry peas.
> My digits click--
> The tips lack even whorls....

She also includes a splendid essay on what she seeks in poetry, and about her influences. She stands outside the usual American modes fostered by Williams and Whitman, and with a rare and crisp intelligence she tells us how. I can't imagine many Americans capable of such supple, intelligent prose.

Since QRL is apparently well-heeled (not only does each poet appearing receive $500 up front, but each manuscript published in the next issue will earn Betty Colladay Awards of $1,000 each), many poets will program their brains to write prize-winning manuscripts, in the sterile modes this journal encourages. What is especially sinister, I feel, is that QRL in nuturing fledgling poets, discourages such poets from experimentation and risk-taking. Academic Sleaze, even when well-written, remains just that. I see most of these poets (and their editors) as ostriches with their heads in the sand--ostrich-angels, if you will, sanitized, without either bungholes or navels. Whitman, thou shoulds't be living at this hour! American verse hath need of thee! My guess is that Walt's manuscripts would be returned within five minutes after the mailman dumped them into the box on Haslet Avenue.

m. peters

SALMAGUNDI

No. 56 (Spring 1982). Editors: Robert and Peggy Boyers. Skidmore College, Saratoga Springs, NY 12866. $9 per year.

SALMAGUNDI's editors like poems with brains and a glossy cryptoclacsticism. If you try to decipher one of their poems and still remain in a quandry, that's just fine--elusiveness passeth for profundity. This issue features "Jaruzelski Winter," by John Peck, a poem as clear as a theorem in physics. What we seem to know is this: Peck packages some old clothes to send to Poland where Gen. Jaruzelski reigns. His "entire people" are "under lock and key." They are "being coldly / tested in the cold." There's a "dwarf" inside Peck, a descendant of those peasants "clustered / around white chapels posted / in stretched fields." An old couple have drafted a protest on paper which flies out the window, useless, and burns by a river. Peck tapes his carton shut--he's sending a scarf, a worn jacket, and greeting. Ashes from the burned paper settle on the package, evoking thoughts of "madness," "honor," "prudence," "patience." The blood of survival, stilled, yet "swirls in the amaranthine / fire of an unstanched flow." This is slick ribbon for the care-package. Pedestrian. There's little zip, flash, or dash. My guess is that the recipient of the scarf and jacket won't comprehend the message either.

Barry Goldensohn's "churchy" woman pleases a boy who sits beside her, a boy "with sheets of hair below his shoulders" and a face "full of dreams of his last battle." Some hoodlums, apparently, were after his cash. There's a frowning husband who has the mind of "an apologist for desperate acts." Not quite so opaque a poet is William Hunt. In "After a Theme By Houdini," a speaker visits the cemetery where Houdini promised to appear after death. But, Hunt reminds us, dead folk "do not return as we were promised / they would."

The best poem is Albert Goldbarth's "Lepidoptera Etc." Details include Mickey Mouse watches, rocking horses, old butterflies. A woman fills Mason jars with momentoes. A neighbor collects pewter swans, another meershaum pipes. In a hospital "day" collects sick people. Goldbarth seems to leave the hospital and write a love poem--a poem to the dying man? His dad? Mr. Toad of Toad Hall? "I don't know what lasts," Goldbarth writes: "but I now how I // want you, how I remember the rising of individual / hairs along your nape like wakened trees in a Disney cartoon."

John Unterecker composes a Yeatsian playlet about a youth in the dunes wanting to slake his soul-thirst; the performance is agile, but conventional. David Kresh is randy as he leaves a lover who arouses him only when he fantasizes about Leslie Caron, celebrates somebody's mother, or extols a stripper ("Ah, the asymmetric / glitter, tinsel eyes"). Wyatt Prunty supplies a pretentious piece ("Uninterrupted days occasion us") written in limping anapests and SALMAGUNDI obscurities. Frank Dwyer's "Prologue," a take on Chaucer and a nun, is earthy; but he spoils "Ploughing on Sunday" with a rash of dull adjectives. Karen Swenson is clear about what Galapagos turtles in the San Diego Zoo mean, and Forest Lawn. Itinerary Poems. Swenson's verses to her folks are better. Mother willed Karen twenty-four pairs of white gloves, all mismatched. Father nagged her as she sought to drown their mutual dislike playing Chopin's "Etudes."

SALMAGUNDI's editors fashion a veneer. Better be dead than brainless.

SHENANDOAH

Vol. XXXII: No. 3 (1981). Poetry Editor: Richard Howard. PO Box 722, Lexington, VA. 24450. $8 per year.

If you don't write iambic lines, or some version thereof, don't send poems here. If you write free verse, you must give the illusion of carefully tooled work and use a few stale Shakespearean breath-whiffs. Once I say this. however, I rush to add that many poems are excellent. There's panache both in style and subject. David Lehman's "The concept of Dread" is intelligent, despite stale ideas and much pretentious language ("this erotic anguish of ours," "a separate grief," "the knowledge of summer in our bones"). John Drury owes much to Walt Whitman's "Out of the Cradle Endlessly Rocking." "The Disappearing Town," echoes Walt's adverb-as-part-of-an-orchestra mode, employing over, past, down, and under, with repetitions, in a verse-sonata about his own boyhood. Here are the usual problems over

mom and dad, sex, and memory. Like Whitman's boy, Drury
throbs towards insight, assisted down life's stream by
further Whitmanic threnodies: "never skating...never
rafting...never climbing...never learning to
swim...afraid of treading water...afraid of opening my
eyes in the river." One sad sack of a kid, right? His
sensitivity, though, made him a poet.

Stuart Friebert's hexameter poem to a retarded
brother is fresh and empathetic, without being
sentimental. David Citno's Thomas Alva Edison writes
Madame Blavatsky of a "disembodied voice" he's trying to
capture via electricity. Michael Rosen sees a child's
world as an elaborate cut-up, stand-out toy. There's a
lovely tentativeness to his vision. Molly Peacock is
amazing. "She Lays" is a stunning poem on female
masturbation:

Secrets have no place in the orchid boat of her
body and old pink brain beneath the willows.

Peacock has style: before she proceeds she makes sure
that her index finger is "beautifully mooned." She also
writes a sonnet about a horrible family picnic. The
Peacock clan "lied, cheated, and shat underneath the
trees / they pissed against." Peacock assures us that
there's "no earthly reason to be horrified / by the fact
that we become like our parents." She should know.

George Bradley writes a pair of stodgy pieces.
Gregory Djanikian spoils "Poisoned Dog" by self-
conscious metaphors; he brings us to a pitch then robs
us by a pretentious image or observation:

I remembered then how my uncle,
once lost in the desert, turned also
but to watch two wild dogs one after another,

honing in on the blood they could scent
and spill, come after him like a dream,
and as the first leapt up to his throat

he caught it with a kick, soccer-style,
and sent both yelping back into the madness
of the desert. . ..

my uncle grateful too...
for what had been spared to go on.
Such magic failed us here: what lay corrupted
was by corruption felled, fallen and held.

A big yes for Terry Stokes' bushy-tailed tone. An aging
man fantasizes about the widow (Death?) he'll meet at

the greenhouse: "She's the Burpee of love / & I'm the sinewy careless ground-wanderer":

> She raises roses as if they were termites.
> She weeds until her fingers crack. Her nails
> leak worms. She is the dream I had this morning,
> & she is by my side tonight. We will die
> together. Nice. You are invited.
> Light on my eyes.

<u>Jordan</u> <u>Smith</u> writes yet another homage to Whitman. The iambs clothe a starchy meditation in "hard-urged words." Smith can't quite believe Walt's dictum that "the smallest sprout shows / There is really no death."

SOUTHERN POETRY REVIEW

Vol. XXII, No. 1 (Spring 1982). Editor: Robert Grey. English Dept., University of North Carolina, Charlotte, NC 28223. $5 per year.

The cover of this current issue is made of a waffled paper, with black titles and a Victorian-appearing colophon. The color is gray, tinged with blue, a sort of foggy sky color. I fear, alas, that this drab color suits the poetry inside. Most of the sixty poets featured write interchangeable works. Stodge is rampant. To show the limitations, I propose to lift a line or two from each poem, fashioning a poem of my own, allowing most of the writers to remain anonymous (rather than tweak them into despair by identifying them). Those few I shall mention rise a cloud or two above the others. Most of these poets are

unknown, and most are Southern. They love reminiscing
over their families and going about gathering up
Wordsworthian sentiments.

SOUTHERN REVIEW POETRY POEM

The moon wavers behind its clouds.
My house cracks its knuckles and my refrigerator
    whispers out a song. Water splashes in the basin.
The earth turns, as imperceptibly as the sonnet used to.

Funeral-figures from Mesopotamia make me cry. Night
  encourages darkness to rise.
I think about a tin bird, as I drink my wine, in
    Andalucia.
The sharp words we spit are like blue pieces of china.
The locks are locked. I Never Really Killed Nobody I
    Don't Think.

A path isn't responsible for wandering off or
    terminating at a briar patch.
I love to put my foot where you've stepped.

James Wright inspires me to delve into the
  mysterious lives of the poor and into Porky
        as he flattens his penis against a window.

I think of the coming night and of
        daddy's black bible
        a jogger riding his mighty and hesitant heart
        an emergency room orderly
        a bear on earth as an Ursa Major up above

        an old fish caught by human hand
        a woman yanking out her hair

I love my kids: a growing son is a growing seed.
Kids grow like fiddleheads in a rock garden.
During the day, kids won't close the doors. At night
they suck their nails and spit them at the stars. My
    kid
My kid is a new ration of days.
Everything is going to fall--leaves, nuts, berries, me.
There's a wasp caught in a storm-sash.

I worry about the true age of the Universe.
A yellow balloon deflates.
I've been hunting my own flesh all these years.
Strange mushrooms spread over startled ground.

Take a good look at Uncle Hal's Ohio farm.
We'd sure like to fish in peace, and not be bothered
  by trembling leaves.
Water plays between the shoulder blades of a day dream.

As I feed the trout they seem to clap hands. I feel
   like clapping too.
What salmon don't go through to spawn!
I was so busy gathering mussels, I didn't see
you were drying your feet on a green bandanna.
Eventually we'll slosh up the dunes and lie in the
   grass.

Coleman lanterns are good for clamming.
The last time I was by this dock, my dad brought me
   fishing.
Now, the old barge aches, and so do I.
An old crab claw creeps from the water to scissor
      my dad's throat.

Conjure a fire to deliver me from this restless dark.
Let's butter and chew a modest life.
I just look at you and see myself 30 years up the road.
I see the unfortunates of Calcutta and think of apples.

I shoulder nude the sea.
Go up and ring the bell.

Rain falls like applesauce on my brick porch. Soon the
      sun moves a terrible tolerance down the streets.
In Kansas, a blind girl is sun-struck. Thank God
      for crabgrass. It cools the pavement between our
      toes.
Later on, Ann's ducks quack up to the chicken wire.
I see myself in a deer's eyes.

It would take a bulldozer to sweep my rooms.
Someday I want my letters back so I can publish them.
You have to know how to act at the end.

You leave me and our daughter, yet the ocean tells us
      our age.
My whole life transpires on a horse.
God, we do love our grandfathers!
That old woman has lizard skin and peels apples in
      curls.
A fecundity of pigs--I've mittened my fingers to spoons.
You must have been sleeping.

Dear Duke, dear John Wayne, our bones glow like neon
   inside our Levis.

This motel won't ever be the same again. I'm at peace.

   Note: This poem may strike readers as not much
different from swinging a scimitar wildly amidst a
passel of heads still attached to bodies. I don't intend

mayhem. To focus on subject-matter, as I have done, at the expense of technique, may not seem fair. But I think it is. For what I said at the outset about grayness is as true of style here as it is of subject-matter. All the poems are in free verse, of varying degrees of competence. Among the best poets are these: Albert Goldbarth, Glenn R. Swetman, Mary Ann Waters, Peter Cooley, Elizabeth Cox, Deborah Woodard, Thomas Heffernan, Mark Halperin, and Gill Holland. On the whole, though, if you expect to find orchids among the flora, you won't find many. Plenty of mullein, dandelions, and an occasional jack-in-the-pulpit or black-eyed susan, peep forth.

m. peters

THE SOUTHERN REVIEW

Vol. 18: No. 2 (April 1982). Editors: Donald E.
Stanford and Lewis P. Simpson. Drawer D, University
Station, Baton Rouge, LA 70893. $7 per year.

THE SOUTHERN REVIEW is clotted with Academic
Sleaze. Not a poem seems touched by anything
transpiring in American poetry since the 1940's when the
Fulbright poem was in, and poets chose motifs dear to
professors--from the Greeks, from Shakespeare, and from
the Sabbatical Tour Abroad.

The oldest poets represented are H. D. (with a
boring "Dodona" and "I Said") and Janet Lewis (if her
two offerings are fair representations of her work, I
can see why she has been neglected). And there is a
feature on the conservative Ann Stanford. Showcased also
is a seven-part work, "Local Winds," by Charles Gullans.
If you read carefully, you will discern references to a
lover's broad back, his playwriting, and his cigarettes.
Why does THE SOUTHERN REVIEW like this poem? Well, it's
rifted with metaphors of love as religion, echoes of
Petrarch, Dante, Shakespeare, and Dante Gabriel
Rossetti. I am grateful, though, that Gullans'
"tomorrows" don't exactly creep in "petty paces":

> I speak to you of many ways of love,
> And in a little while, we shall lie down,
> And we will learn of all of them. Tonight,
> Tomorrow, and tomorrow, we are flesh,
> We are incarnate names; and we speak tongues
> Of revelation, flame upon our lips.
> And we are in one place with one accord.
> Turn to me now, and I will worship here.
> I am so filled to utterance that I
> Propound divinity from sacred texts
> Of brow and lips.

There's a sanitized kiss or two ("the gift of tongues")
and a whitened-off sexual moment transpiring amidst very
white sheets:

> Dear friend, unravel this,
> How well we fit in this asexual,

Least usable position, back to front,
My hand around and light upon your chest,
And tapping out the rhythm of a thought,
My nose deep in the fragrance of your hair,
The comfort of your skin.

Later on, in "Jacob's Ladder," poet and friend "know the
youthful god," "Eros the Terrible," who climbs into
their bed, folds them "in his wide embrace" and is
sexually trashy. (Or so the implication is).
"Something is surely coming to an end," pontificates
Gullans. Not far ahead we hear Yeats' "violence upon
the roads," etc. I turn the page expecting more.

But I find less. I meet poets (most of whom shall
remain nameless) interchangeable one with the other.
Predictable literary allusions abound, ones that
academics spew forth in lit classes: Ulysses, the Sirens
(they turn up in two poems), Caligula, Orpheus,
Kirkegaard, Zeus, Hymettus, the Nereids--"chthonic"
offerings all, on the altar of Academic Sleaze. One
poet, David Middleton, knows his Tennyson pretty well:
his "Sirens" is an impressive echoing of detritus from
Tennyson's more flamboyant monologues: "swooning awake,"
"unshrouded wisdom," "essential night," "murmuring
time."

Opening lines overtly Shakespearean in their
orotundity, pretentiousness, and elevation sound like
exercises for a typing-class: "The recent storms'
detritus banks the dune"; "How many times I've dreamed
you here, the black"; "Ascent is simple where the
tourists are"; and "A center of the world: in power
once." Occasionally, a poem works, as does Suzanne J.
Doyle's "My Mother's Jewels," fashioned of seven triplet
stanzas plus a concluding couplet. The terza rima is a
demanding form. There are surprises: the woman's mother
pinched fireflies in half and affixed them to her
daughter's fingers. She tore off "the lucent body at
the wing" and wore "the pulsing globe." (Sniff that
Shakespearean turn). Doyle likes rhymed poems. She
loves Sleaze Phrases too: "consecrated host," "some
celestial, mechanistic will" (thanks, T. Hardy), and
"meaning's adumbration." Pearl Sherry spins off poems
about a skull and a man as an hourglass. She's the one
who writes about Nereids and "chthonic offerings."

When Joyce Carol Oates appears, I am relieved.
She, at least, must read contemporary poets--or so I
assume. But she supplies no evidence she does.
"Nightless Nights" is one of those Academics-On-Leave
poems. Oates is in the far north somewhere--it is day
all night long. The zest she spends caressing vapid
gerunds may say she's been up to no good with swan-

necks: "dreaming," "unceasing," "scuttling," "unsleeping." Her "High-Wire Artist" is a monologue in the warmed-over manner of Robert Browning. She echoes that old fart of a Bishop ordering his tomb, one of the most admired (and taught) of all personages in nineteenth-century poems. Here is Browning: "Hours and long hours in the dead night, I ask / Do I live, am I dead?" Here is Oates: "Nights of getting through nights. / Often I forget: am I dead now, or still alive." Pick the better effort. Oates concludes with bathos: "It is not God that beckons, only the sawdust."

The poetry winds off with Ann Hayes, inspired by academic trips to Cluny, Paris, Chartres, and the Jungfrau mountains. She even writes on dolphins, guided, probably, by Yeats' "Byzantium," another much-taught piece. But, wait! We're not through: Jeffrey Goodman turns in three Ben Jonsonian epigrams and yet another Hamlet's skull poem.

As for the reviews of poetry and prose: four books are published by Farrar, Straus, and Giroux; one by Knopf; one by Dead Lines press. Conclusion: academics and their editors have always been, and probably always will be, closet-cases.

TELEPHONE

No. 17 (August 1981). Editor: Maureen Owen. 109 Dunk
Rock Road, Guilford, CT 06437. $7 for 2 issues.

        Fatigued with reading literary magazines deserving
more bruises for flatulence than kisses for vitality, I
sought for at least one I might celebrate. I had heard
good things about TELEPHONE. I plunked down seven bucks
for two recent issues, thinking to find verve,
iconoclasm, vibrancy. TELEPHONE is fat, almost 150
pages, with some 75 poets and artist represented.
There's a nice tipped-in cartoon, in the Steve Canyon
manner, of a dude electrified by his telephone receiver,
and a scary HA HA HA filling in space. Nice.

        But what are the poems like? There's a mix of
unknowns and knowns. What wearies is the lack of many
distinctive voices. Cuteness palls. Much tonal
insipidity. The tone is set by Rachelle Bijou (a
pseudonym?) in a fantasized St.Mark's Poetry Department
Store. Here are some of Ms. Bijou's cute pearls: "for
the ultimate in stereo sound / check out the works of
Jackson MacLow." Over in WORDS A LA CARTE you'll find
"wares" by Lyn Hejinian, Clark Coolidge, and Bruce
Andrews. Near the JOHN ASHBERY GALLERY, James Schuyler
has his HOME SHOP. Here you'll find thrilling "nascent
what-have-yous." There's Anselm Hollo, F. T. Prince,
and Yuki Hartman in THE INTERNATIONAL SHOP. Lita Hornick
is on the third floor, in FANTASTIC FURS. And in the
surf-shop, CALIFORNIA DREAMIN', you'll find Tom Clark,
Joanne Kyger, and Robert Duncan. This is dreadful!
Belly-buttons stuffed with cheese!

        Tom Weigel, at least, is modest, and says that his
poems require "only scribbles" and "lots of breath."
Emily Borenstein lies "dead of expectation," her "wet
swollen poem" lying nearby "prone / like an edematous
brain." John P. Trump shows his tame-card, avowing that
Gerald Stern is "gentle / As soft as the chrysanthemums
/ he talks about." Special pleading? Trump arrives to
"lay low in the lilies / and love the light and the
darkness as one." Ulysses A. Pinchon writes while
"staring at Al Jarreau's album cover." Susan Roberts
girl-chatters about a party:

            as pretty as poppy can be be be
            eyes up face
            thump heart   eyes   move around.

Rose Lesniak eschews good grammar and writes about cows
that "make you smell." She's "smashed on the IRT."

Tom Savage's "Androgyny" sounds wise: "why not just call all men women / since that name contains both?" Al Simons opines that if you're a parakeet "nobody cares"; just beware of "the asshole sparrow." John Paul supplies a benedication (papal?) suitable for most of the poems in TELEPHONE:

> A fine mixture
> Outrage fish eggs
>
> Childish wit
> and cheap wine.

What poems are worth reading? Derek Pell's "Don't Wake Rimbaud," despite boring line-lengths, has energy. Mary Abrams' "Post-Partum Blues" gives the simple-minded nose-thumb to the trivia most of these poets write. Her style is utterly primer-like:

> She doesn't kiss him goodbye.
>
> She kisses him goodbye.
>
> The baby wakes and cries.
>
> She goes and gets the baby, packs a bag,
> grabs the charge cards, the savings book, and
> the check book. She picks quarters out of the
> loose change jar. She gets dressed. She changes
> the baby, makes herself a bologna sandwich,
> wraps it neatly in tinfoil, and waits for the taxi.
>
> She goes to the room and gets the baby.
>
> She gives him a bottle of vodka and juice.
>
> She nurses him.

The poem oscillates around the possibilities in a tacky domestic tragedy. The spots on the dice don't change-- the combinations do. Dick Barnes writes an unforgettable "Doctor Knows Best," where an old Tennessee lady allows the doctor to cut off her frozen feet. Chuang Tzu and Hui Tzu exchange thoughts on Jesus Christ, that "country boy" who cruciflew up to the sky. Jana Harris writes with pizazz about "how men get hard and callous." Robert Hershon contributes modest poems: it's enough, he writes, "merely" to be "faithful / to our favorite candy bars."

Emilie Glen wades into men who have "water on the balls"--she writes music-hall riffs, tacky, great for

singing. An old wheelchair lady across the hall dies
("the body," writes Glen, "must have its paper work").
Here is the whole of "BALLS":

```
Water on the balls
     musical
                mystical
     good for a laugh
Water    water
     water on
water on the balls
                water chestnuts
Now he has confessed to water on the balls
     can he touch off my fireworks
confessed to another woman
     who came giggling to me
the balls    the balls
     water on the balls
which one does he love more
     the one he tells    one he doesn't tell
sounds minty chlorophylled   field flower
     water    water on the balls
```

I also liked Leslie Adrienne Miller's "Pen Drawing for
Harper's Young People," Guy Beining's "stoma" poems, and
Steve Abbott's celebration of Genet's "smelly shoes" and
sexism. TELEPHONE, why not go for a shorter mag, with
more quality? Move to Dumont, Minnesota and settle for
a slimmer phone-book, without the Yellow Pages.

THE VIRGINIA QUARTERLY REVIEW

Vol. 58: No. 2 (Spring 1982). 1 West Range,
Charlottesville, VA 22903. Poetry Consultant: Gregory
Orr. $10 per year.

The poems here are decent. No leaking taps. No
funk. No cracked mirrors. Everything nicely tooled.
Better Homes and Gardens poem-interiors. Most poems
assembled by a generation of poets now in their early
forties. That's roughly the Poetry Consultant's age, I
would guess. The least interesting writer (let's get to
the weak stuff first) is Irving Feldman. He lards on
the clichés as if high-cholesterol spreads were still in
style. The writing is very Jamesian, Ashberyan, very
trivial:

                                    --it had to go
without saying--that she was his superior.
Let him elevate that noble brow of his
in the salon of the famous babies, she knew
--just didn't she--who was the lion's hairdresser!
Oh, it might have been restful there beside him
--so slow, so unwitting--she'd have napped a bit,
but the injustice kept picking into her heart,
and she muttered How dare he! How dare he!

Two poems by Cynthia Huntington follow, both slack in
the extreme. "Here Come The Men My Mother Warned Me Of"
is an expansive riff on the Lady Chatterly Syndrome--
workingmen are much better fucks than men "who open
doors and dial telephones." The second poem,
"Migraine," wallows in pain:

                                    We can keep our pain;
we can keep dying. When the body dies it grows
       stiff
and swells with all it had kept to itself. Finally
the skin bursts and it all rushes out, stinking,
       and then
the body lets everything in. Grass, earth, other
       bodies.

Now, that's enough to charm the worst migraine.

Greg Kuzma's "Hands" is an example of Kuzma's
messing around, writing a poem without much evident
need. He displays a "poky thumb with big magnificence";
it's been smashed by a hammer. Two by Michael Cadmus
are OK. I like it that he loves Los Angeles and isn't
afraid to say so. I wish though he'd forgotten about
his old dad sitting up "sleepless beside a light." John
Vernon contributes "A Fly." The last stanza borders on
sentiment rather than insight. "Ashes" is better. A
pail of ashes falls into a frozen creek. Months later,
Vernon spots the pail where the creek now whirls around
it: "Suddenly it's spring."

The last poet is Dave Smith. His "Dry Ice" is a
messy dream intended, probably, to be more fearsome than
it is. Its one of those "let's return to gradeschool"
poems. L'il Dave wasn't much into chemistry, and mostly
lay on the floor dreaming, apart from the other boys who
were interested in chemistry and boy-things. Poet as
Sensitive Plant. Dry ice in his mouth shakes him loose.
He's a "sizzle and lick of meat." A "big voice," a god-
father figure, shouts at him, lays on "the blade of his
hand," and sends Davie scurrying down to the "room of
the rocks" (fancy way of saying "basement") where he
howls in the dark and, I guess, becomes a poet. The

"dead" down there spookily look at him from the stone walls. They urge him to <u>speak, speak.</u> They give him his tongue.

In "Toy Trains in the Landlord's House," the Smith family lives in a house once owned by an old Judge. In the basement of "raw stone" are a dirty old train and lots of sooted tables filled with town, depot, and countryside. We endure yet another of Smith's semi-scary, boy-visions: the old Judge watches Smith "in this crypt," demanding to know "what unscheduled / interruption breaks before him now." Shamed and fearsome, Smith leaves, only to imagine the old man, night after night, appearing to "keep some few / workable wheels rolling." Then, in a leap that flops like a splattered frog, we learn that the Judge's problem is Smith's. The metaphysical implications are sentimental: "the homeless dead," lodged in the basement, have "papery faces." Masks? A black racer-train sweeps their "heartbeats" away (a modern Charon's ferry boat?). Smith, "like a man condemned / to see what we are flashed past," is "unable to rise." Smith loses me. The metaphysical stuff isn't earned. It seems written with backward glances at the easier parts of Dante. Also, Smith's combinations of the pretentious (that old disease, Momentosity) and clichéd phrases (viz., "into the light of our living") betray Smith. Yet, even as a failure, Smith provides better fare than we get from most of these other poets.

WORMWOOD REVIEW

(Nos. 80 and 85, 1980 and 1982). Editor: Marvin Malone, PO Box 8840, Stockton, CA 95208. $5 for individuals. $6 for institutions per year.

<u>Poetry should be about things. What things is poetry about since 1815? The poet's mistress is cruel to him. The poet fears he is going to die or fears he is not going to die. Rather like a sea sickness. The world is a fearful emptiness, but birds and flowers grant some little consolation. Perhaps next year there will</u>

be a new subject, but I think most poets have
their elegies on Napoleon waiting.

--Anthony Burgess, ABBA ABBA

Through an imagined conversation between the
nineteenth-century poet Belli and a Professor, Giovanni
Gulielmi, Burgess remarks on the dual strands in nearly
all poetry--the conservative strand satirized above
(symbolized by John Keats, a character in this amazing
novella), and the earthy, vulgarian strand present in
Belli's own poetry. He even writes a poem on the
foreskin of Jesus.

What, you ask, does this have to do with Marvine
Malone's WORMWOOD REVIEW? Plenty. And since the
magazine has just seen its 94th issue, a publishing
record extending over twenty-three years, it is indeed
one that shouldn't be overlooked. WORMWOOD REVIEW
reflects the exclusive tastes of one man, Malone, a
professor of pharmacology and toxicology at the
University of the Pacific, Stockton. His tastes, as we
shall see, reflect the Bellian rather than the Keatsian
strand in poetry.

From the start, Malone knew the writing he liked.
In "The Why and Wherefore of Wormwood," to appear in
DECEMBER MAGAZINE, he lists ten guidelines he follows:
"(i) avoid publishing oneself and personal friends, (ii)
avoid being a local magazine and strive for a national
and international audience (iii) seek unknown talents
rather than establishment or fashionable authors (iv)
encourage originality by working with and promoting
authors capable of extending the existing patterns of
Amerenglish literature (v) avoid all cults and
allegiances...accept the fact that magazine content is
more important than format in the long run (vii) presume
a literature audience and try to make the mag readable
from the first page to the last (viii) restrict the
number of pages to no more than 40 per issue since only
the insensitive and the masochistic can handle more
pages at one sitting (ix) pay bills on time and don't
expect special favors in honor of the muse, and lastly
and most importantly (x) don't become too serious and
righteous." And he adds this astute observation:
"Ignoring the above ten commandments appears to lay the
ground for a mag's self-destruction. Very few little
mags are terminated by outside forces--they self-
destruct!"

Malone's poets (and he's published his favorites
over and over) are earthy, sexual, street-wise, rich in
failures, iconoclastic. They follow a line of poetry

whose genealogy includes Chaucer (of the fabliaux),
Villon, Shakespeare (when he was bawdy), Dante,
Rabelais, Swift, Baudelaire, Whitman, and Belli. This
strand has always been antithetical to Piss-Elegant
Writing as admired by the traditional muse and academics
with their sucker-mouths syphoning up poets, encouraging
the latter to produce poet-toad mush.

The 80th number of WORMWOOD is a reprise of the
poets who've appeared often over the decades. Each
issue contains a Chapbook Supplement, inserted,
featuring a specific poet, some old, some new. A
reading is illuminating. Charles Bukowski heads the
list. In fact, Malone was publishing C. B. before nary
an ermine-trimmed poetry-tippet was tossed his way.
Judson Crews has appeared sixteen times, in two
Supplements. Gloria Kenison who liked word-lists (she
is deceased) was in 22 issues (2 supplements). Gerald
Locklin, the Laureate of Long Beach, has spread his
inimitable works over 29 issues (4 Supplements), a
record surpassing Bukowski's. Steve Richmond has
written gagaku for ten years, from Santa Monica. Phil
Weidman (20 issues, 1 Supplement) celebrates the fact
that if he had an aura it would be "piss yellow." He's
a prole who celebrates issues native to the species.
He's writing about "free time":

    Got to cultivate
    it carefully
    make it pay
    while it lasts.
    Waste is the
    grey reaper
    of middle age.

The Madonna of the Wormwoodian stables is Lyn Lifshin
who whinnies through 20 issues and 3 Supplements).
Contrary to her reputation, Lifshin isn't always in
heat, although she does contribute occasional no-holds
barred sex poems. She can write unpretentious lyrics.
Here is one:

    Letter

    Everything is
    all dripping and
    fog. Even the white
    stars on the dog
    wood are little
    platters full of
    rain. Tuesday seems
    12 weeks away
    the cherries will
    be ripe by then

the columbine be
the color of skin
with a little rose.

Then we have Pasadena's gift to poetry, <u>Ron Koertge</u>.
He's one of the funniest, most sardonically winsome of
Malone's poets. He rings in (he's appeared in 14 earlier
issues, 3 Supplements) with poems on Lassie's wedding
night, the wonders of slipper sox, sunglasses, and his
own genealogy. Here's the close of "Functions of Body
Hair":

This is what the hair on someone's ass is for,
the tickly wisps around the nipple, those shoulders
and backs, each a tiny pampas.

It all lets you know that this is not the funny
papers and that someone is about to do something
human.

Scrutinizing WORMWOOD, one suspects that Malone all by
himself has nurtured what amounts to a California
School. All except Lifshin, Kenison, and Crews (he's
from Albuquerque, so sort of counts) are Californian.
One has the image of a vast warty face with Charles
Bukowski as the primary carbuncle, with other wens and
wenlettes in planetary positions around his.

Issue 80 is a showcase issue, featuring as it does
eight regulars. No other issue of the mag is like it--
for all others include unknown poets. Malone prides
himself on such discoveries. His is not a closed
magazine. (Most of the work in AMERICAN POETRY REVIEW,
I am told, is solicited by the editors). The host of
fruitful new talents Malone has encouraged is
impressive, sufficient to burn up all the ergot-riddled
work in lesser journals. WORMWOOD #85, for example, has
five new poets among nine. <u>Eric Grow</u>, a new writer,
contributes this:

A NATURAL

Just as soon as I get
a steel pin in my shoulder,
and my teeth straightened,
some contact lenses fitted,
and my nose fixed
I'm going to start capitalizing
on my natural superiority

Here is <u>Nichola Manning</u>'s "ONE MORE ROUND FOR
HIROSHIMA":

I've always wanted to do it with
my mother. Fly to Australia,
that is, with her in the baggage hold,
and me in the first class with

earphones on, listening to
something quiet and undemanding.
And, possibly, by the time the plane
touches down in Sydney, she'll have
been dropped on Hiroshima.

You get the idea: Malone is on the search for fresh,
iconoclastic writers. He advises that writers who wish
to submit work first read his magazine. Otherwise, you
may waste postage. WORMWOOD is a good read. The only
magazines that compare in vitality and spunk are KAYAK,
LITTLE CAESAR, CHELSEA, CONTACT II, BARNEY, and SOUP.

THE BLACK AND BLUE GUIDE AWARDS

CATEGORY ONE:

CATEGORY TWO:

Chelsea, Kayak, Little Caesar, Wormwood Review

CATEGORY THREE:

Abraxas, Boxcar, Kenyon Review, Poetry Now,
Shenandoah   0

CATEGORY FOUR:

Antaeus, Chicago Review, Georgia Review, Hudson
Review, Iowa Review, New Yorker, Poetry, Quarterly
Review of Literature, Salmagundi, Telephone, Virginia
Quarterly Review

CATEGORY V:

American Poetry Review, Field, Ohio Review, Poetry
Northeast, Pushcart Prizes, Southern Poetry Review,
Southern Review

INDEX OF NAMES

TOPICS INDEX